Barnstaple Fair
Pears

RECIPE ON PAGE 86

THE FESTIVE TABLE

Celebrating the seasons with traditional recipes

JANE PETTIGREW

PAVILION

For ARF with much love

First published in 1990 by
PAVILION BOOKS LIMITED
196 Shaftesbury Avenue, London WC2H 8JL

Text copyright © Jane Pettigrew 1990
Illustrations copyright © Moira Macgregor 1990
Designed by Janet James

A CIP catalogue record for this book is available
from the British Library

ISBN 1 85145 460 6

10 9 8 7 6 5 4 3 2 1

Printed in England
by Clays Ltd, St Ives Plc

CONTENTS

Acknowledgements

With thanks to all the people who sent me recipes, to Women's Institutes
around the country, and to all
my friends on whom I tried out the recipes.

The following recipes are still in print elsewhere
and I am grateful to the copyright holders for their
permission to use them:

Hop Pickers' Cake was taken from *Folk in Kent* ed.
Jack Hamilton, a magazine of the English Folk
Dance and Song Society in Kent.

Goosnargh Cakes came from *More Old Lancashire
Recipes* by Joan Poulson (publisher: Hendon Publishing Company).

Herring Pie came from Suzanne Whooley's *My
Grandmother's Cookery Book* (publisher: Shearwater
Press Limited).

Potato Pudding was taken from *Welsh Country
Cookery* by Bobby Freeman (publisher: Y Lolfa).

Vegetarian Mincemeat is featured in *Recipes from
Wrawby* produced by the Humberside Women's
Institute.

Duck in Cider and Jugged Steak both came from
Traditional West Country Cookery by Theodora
Fitzgibbon (Fontana), and by the same author *A
Taste of Yorkshire* (Pan) provided me with Love
Feast Cake.

INTRODUCTION

One of my favourite old recipe books is Florence White's *Good Things in England*. I was browsing through it one day, fascinated as usual by all the information and folklore that emerge from the recipes, and particularly by the stories about recipes that were cooked for specific occasions around England, when I realized that there were probably many more traditional recipes not in Florence White's book but still being cooked around Britain. I decided to do some research and see what I could find. This book is a selection of the most interesting and appealing of the recipes that I came across.

Our idea today of festive food is very different from that of previous centuries. Today we have easy access to food products from all over the world and we have the money to buy them. We tend to plan menus based not only on what is in season but also around ideas of texture, colour, variety of taste, what will impress, and so on. And we enjoy special meals prepared for special occasions knowing that we shall also eat well tomorrow and the day after that. In medieval days, and probably earlier, feasting was enjoyed by the majority of the population in the full knowledge that there would be an inevitable return to a very simple diet, and possibly to a fast, immediately afterwards. Life tended to oscillate between feasting and fasting, and depended largely on the seasons and the harvest. The wealthy landed gentry ate well most of the time, and gave their surplus to the poor, but most people were lucky to have anything much at all to eat. Their diet consisted mainly of bread, vegetables and pottage, boiled up from peas and pulses. At times of celebration anything more would have been a treat. Communal feasts normally took place on major religious and pastoral occasions such as May Day, Whitsuntide, mid-summer, harvest time, Michaelmas, Martinmas, Christmas, weddings, christenings and funerals. Many of the church festivities that provided the occasion for feasting developed from pagan festivals that had been adopted and adapted by the early Christians. Very often the eating of special foods on such occasions also had a pagan origin. Eccles cakes and Banbury cakes are just two examples of recipes that have descended from pagan foods and are still popular today.

The church was, of course, the focal point of the community, and of events in the natural cycle of life such as weddings, christenings, funerals, the harvest, and Christmas. The nave of the church acted as a sort of village hall and all sorts of activities took place there and in the churchyard – not only worship, but also church revels, fairs, markets, morris dancing, bear baiting and feasting. The only part of the church that was sacred and used only for services was the chancel.

The church calendar itself is a mixture of old pastoral pagan festivals and more recent Christian ones. Before Christianity two natural rural calendars operated, the agricultural and the pastoral. The agricultural calendar is still evident in the four quarter days that still operate in Scotland: Lady Day (25 March), Midsummer (24 June), Michaelmas (29 September) and Christmas. The pastoral calendar was marked out by four different quarter days: Imbolc (1 February), the lambing festival, Beltane (1 May) when new grazing land was ready, Lugnasad (1 August) when shearing was finished and fairs were held, and Samhain (1 November) when the flocks were rounded up and surplus animals were slaughtered. This pastoral calendar is the older of the two but was submerged by the agricultural. The old feast days were taken over and renamed. Imbolc became Candlemas Day, Beltane became May Day, Lugnasad became Lammastide, the festival of the first fruit, and Samhain became Martinmas. This agricultural calendar was in due course taken over by the church and the old festivals continued as before, enabling the peasants to take all their traditional holidays (holy days) without upsetting church laws.

During the sixteenth, seventeenth and eighteenth centuries patterns of diet stabilized and gradually all but the very poor came to have access to more regular supplies of dairy produce, vegetables, bread, a little meat and perhaps fish. The normal practice at feast times in most families was to save a special cut of meat or even to kill an animal specially for the occasion – spring lamb or veal for the special Sundays in Lent, a good side of beef for the harvest supper – or to use whatever produce was available and make it special by adding a little butter, cream, herbs, spices or alcohol. Most of the festive cakes of the past were nothing more than a piece of ordinary bread dough enriched with eggs, dried fruits, spices and butter. During the nineteenth century many people became more affluent, and so could afford more and better ingredients. It was during this period that simple festive fare began to develop into more elaborate recipes. Simple cakes based on bread dough were made instead with baking powder and more eggs, spices and fruit; cooking methods changed with the development of the kitchen range and gas and electricity supplies; and, with industrialization, many of the special rural dishes became more generally available, and through becoming more everyday lost their significance. And so, over the years, we have lost many of our traditional recipes or, if the dishes are still cooked, we have forgotten the links that they originally had with festive occasions.

I have been able to trace the origins and significance of some recipes, but I feel that there are probably far more local and regional specialities that have an interesting history, and I would love to hear from anybody around the British Isles who can give more information. I am extremely grateful to all those who sent me recipes for this collection and I apologize for the fact that lack of space and the risk of repetition have not allowed me to include more examples. People have been very generous with both recipes and family tales of when and why certain foods were eaten, and I have been fascinated by the information that has emerged. I hope the book will be useful and interesting, and will help to save at least some of our traditional dishes.

January

17 St Antony
21 St Agnes
24 St Timothy

February

1 St Brigid, or Bride, of Kildare
2 The Purification of the Blessed Virgin Mary (Candlemas Day)
5 St Agatha
12 St Ethelwald of Lindisfarne
14 St Valentine

March

1 St David
8 St John of God
17 St Patrick
19 St Joseph

April

23 St George
25 St Mark
28 St Paul of the Cross

May

4 Martyrs of England and Wales
8 The Apparition of St Michael
27 St Bede The Venerable

June

2 St Erasmus
5 St Boniface
9 St Columba, or Colmcille
11 St Barnabas
24 Feast of the Nativity of John the Baptist
26 St John and St Paul
29 St Peter the Apostle
30 Commemoration of St Paul

July

2 Visitation of The Blessed Virgin Mary
9 St Thomas More
22 St Mary Magdalen
25 St James the Greater
26 St Anne
31 St Ignatius of Loyola

August

5 St Oswald
10 St Lawrence
12 St Clare
24 St Bartholomew

September

8 Feast of the Nativity of The Blessed Virgin Mary
21 St Matthew
29 St Michael (Michaelmas)

October

4 St Francis of Assissi
12 St Wilfrid of York
13 St Edward The Confessor
18 St Luke
25 St Crispin and St Crispinian

November

1 All Saints
2 All Souls
3 St Winifred
11 St Martin (Martimas)
22 St Cecelia, or Cecily
23 St Clement
30 St Andrew

December

3 St Francis Xavier
21 St Thomas the Apostle
25 Feast of the Nativity of Jesus Christ
26 St Stephen
27 St John the Evangelist
29 St Thomas of Canterbury

Simnel Cake

RECIPE ON PAGE 24

SPRING

The first and greatest of the spring festivals is Easter, the second most important date in the Christian calendar. The prelude to Easter is Lent, the period of forty days, not counting Sundays, from Ash Wednesday to Easter Saturday. For Christians, it marks the forty days that Jesus spent in the wilderness preparing himself for his public ministry, and is a time of fasting and prayer. In the past there were always four or five days of boisterous festivities before the period of discipline and and fasting began, and the Thursday before Lent was suitably known as Carnival or Mad Thursday. During the fast, meat, eggs, fat and other animal products were forbidden, so those last few days of celebration were a time for eating up any of the prohibited foods that would not keep until Easter.

The Monday before the start of Lent was known in some regions as Collop Monday, after the 'collops' or thick slices of bacon or salt pork that were fried with eggs for the evening meal. In other areas, the same day was named Peasen or Paisen Monday on account of the soup made from dried peas and ham or pork stock that was traditionally eaten.

Shrove Tuesday, the last day before the fast began, was called Fassens or Fastens Eve, and was a half-holiday for schoolchildren and apprentices. In many towns it was a day for village sports, games and traditional pastimes such as archery and football. On Shrove Tuesday morning the 'Shriving Bell' rang to call villagers to church to confess and be shriven of their sins. In more recent years the same bell was rung to warn housewives to begin to prepare their pancake batter, as this is also Pancake Day. Pancakes were cooked to use up surplus eggs and fat, and are today the only surviving Lenten dish that is still generally known and cooked throughout Britain. They may have been a development of the small wheatcakes eaten at early spring festivals in pre-Christian days, and in Scotland oat bannocks, which are closer still to those early wheatcakes, are the familiar dish for Shrove Tuesday. They are eaten with a soup-like beef stew called Matrimonial Brose and the day is often known as Bannock Day or Brose and Bannock Day. The brose traditionally has a wedding ring dropped into it and whoever finds the ring will be the first to marry.

Over the years the making and eating of pancakes has acquired a folklore of its own in most regions of Britain, and customs vary widely. At Olney in Buckinghamshire an annual race is run through the streets, from the market place to the church, with contestants carrying their frying pan and pancake. The pancake must be tossed at the beginning and end of the race and the winner has the honour of serving his or her pancake to the bell ringers. At Westminster School in London the boys scramble for a single pancake that is specially cooked by the school chef and tossed over a high iron bar that divides the upper and lower school. In Ireland housewives play a trick on new young wives by sending them off in search of a non-existent pancake sieve.

Ash Wednesday, the first day of Lent, is so called after the practice in the early Christian church of sprinkling ashes on the heads of those who showed true sorrow for their sins, or of marking a cross in ashes on the forehead to remind man of his mortality. A modern confusion over the day's name has arisen in some northern regions owing to a popular dish of hashed potatoes that was traditionally served on 'Hash Wednesday'.

The fourth Sunday of Lent was called Mid-Lent, Mothering Sunday or Simnel Sunday. It was a recognized day of relaxation from the Lenten fast and was therefore also called Refreshment Sunday. Families attended a special service at the mother church, then enjoyed a festive meal together. Although simnel cakes are now more often eaten at Easter, they were originally baked for Mothering Sunday. The other significant name for this fourth Sunday in Lancashire was Braggot Sunday after a traditional drink called braggot or bragget (also bragwort, braggat or bracket) originally made by fermenting ale and honey together. Later the honey was replaced by sugar and spices.

An important dish for Mid-Lent was furmenty (also called frumity, fomenty, fru-

mety, furmity and all sorts of other variations). It is probably the oldest recorded English dish and takes its name from the Latin *frumentum*, meaning corn. It is made from fresh wheat, steeped for several hours in water or milk over a very low heat. In its earliest, simple form it was served as an accompaniment to meats such as venison and porpoise, and records show that it was served as part of the second course of a meal for Henry IV in the fourteenth century. Later it was commonly eaten as an everyday dish mixed with milk and honey, and for special occasions such as Mid-Lent, harvest time and Christmas it was boiled up with dried fruits or plums and sugar and spices.

The fifth Sunday, Passion Sunday, marks the beginning of the two weeks of Passion-tide, which ends on Easter Sunday. It is also called Care Sunday (or Carl, Cair, Carline, Carling, Caris, Kyarlin) because of its associations with sorrow and mourning. It was the custom for centuries in many parts of Britain to eat dried peas, or carlings, on this day. They were soaked overnight and then fried in butter and served with salt and pepper or sometimes vinegar. It is unclear whether the day gave its name to the food or vice versa, but peas and beans have been associated with death and mourning since the days of the ancient Greeks, who believed that they contained the souls of the dead.

The sixth Sunday is Palm Sunday, widely known until the late 1930s as Fig Sunday or Fig Pudding Day. The reason for this is probably the story in the Gospels of how Jesus cursed a barren fig tree on his way to Jerusalem. In many regions, particularly the Midlands, the Home Counties, Wiltshire and Yorkshire, fig puddings and pies were the standard dishes for Palm Sunday. Other Palm Sunday specialities include rice pudding in Kent, and in Northampton, little pies made with brandy, candied peel and hard-boiled eggs.

In the days when fasting was strictly observed, fish and vegetables formed the staple diet during Lent, and only children and invalids were allowed to eat a little meat. As religious observance slackened, so eating habits became more flexible and relaxed, and popular dishes came to include some of the forbidden foods, particularly eggs. This is why so many of the recipes in this section use meat, eggs and fat despite the earlier rules of abstinence.

The fasting and prayer of Lent culminate at Easter, with special church services, feasting and festivities. The name 'Easter' derives ultimately from the Saxon *oster*, meaning to rise, which links it with the rising of the sun after the winter to give longer daylight hours, and also from Eastre or Eostre, the name of the Saxon goddess who was worshipped at this season. When the Anglo-Saxons converted to Christianity, the old pagan spring rituals became attached to and absorbed by the new Christian festival, and April was always called Eostermonath. Easter falls between 25 March and 25 April, the precise date depending on the full moon that occurs on or after the spring equinox.

Good Friday commemorates the day of Jesus's crucifixion. 'Good' originally meant holy, and Easter, Christmas and Shrovetide at the start of Lent were known as Good-tides. All sorts of superstitions and beliefs are associated with Good Friday. In some regions it was generally believed that it was a day on which the earth should not be disturbed, while in others people held that anything planted on Good Friday would produce an excellent crop, for this was the one day when the earth was completely good and holy, because the power of Satan had been overcome by the death of Christ. In most country areas it was believed

that eggs laid on Good Friday had the power to extinguish fire, and that bread baked on that day would not go mouldy but would ensure good luck in the house throughout the coming year. A freshly baked miniature loaf or bun was often hung above the stove or hearth to ward off evil, to protect the house from fire and to prevent further batches of bread from going bad.

Of all the things to be baked on Good Friday the place of honour went to hot cross buns. Originally made from left-over dough used to make the sacramental loaves for Good Friday services, these special cakes were always marked with a cross. They were thought to have curative powers, and at least one bun was kept back from the batch so that crumbs from it could be used in home remedies for the family and livestock during the year.

As Fridays throughout the year were always fast or meatless days, Good Friday, in Lent, was doubly so. For those who could afford it or who had access to it, fish therefore became the main food. In some parts of Britain there would be special Good Friday trips to the rivers or coasts to collect shellfish and catch fresh fish, and in others salt fish was usually available. Otherwise the diet was much the same as during the rest of Lent, with dishes made from vegetables, herbs, oats and pulses. In Lancashire and the Lake District a fig soup made with ale was eaten before the main course.

Celebrations on Easter Sunday usually start with a breakfast of painted boiled eggs. The custom of eating, decorating and giving eggs on this day can be traced back to most ancient civilizations. To Egyptians, Persians, Greeks, Gauls and Romans alike the egg was a symbol of the universe, the work of a supreme power or divinity, and an old European myth represented the sun of spring as a red or golden egg. The egg is also a symbol of fertility and new life and, like all meat and other animal products, was forbidden from the diet of Christians during Lent.

The decorating of eggs has a long history in Britain. The Easter accounts for the royal household during Edward I's reign (1239–1307) show that 450 eggs (costing eighteen pence altogether) were stained by boiling in dye or covered with gold leaf to be given to members of the household. All over Britain games involving decorated eggs are still played on Easter Sunday. They are rolled down hills, smashed together like conkers, thrown in the air and caught, begged, hidden and hunted and shaken together in baskets until three winning, uncracked eggs are left. In some northern counties, Pace-eggers, young men with blackened faces and dressed in fancy costume, would act out a drama or stylized battle before taking round a basket to collect eggs and money. The word 'pace' derives from the Hebrew 'passover' and was much more commonly used in the past than 'Easter'. In Scotland until quite recently, Easter Sunday was known as Pass, Paiss or Pasch Sunday.

Easter Sunday was (and still is) a time for celebration and feasting, when traditional family meals would be based around roast spring lamb or veal or sometimes bacon or pork. This would be followed by custards and cheesecakes, to use up the glut of eggs laid during Lent and the milk that was always plentiful in the spring. The feast of special foods was a reminder that winter was over and the new season of foods and crops was beginning. In Cornwall a split-pea soup was made with the tail of the winter salted pig to symbolize the passing of winter and with it the need for salted meat.

In Irish towns and villages Easter Sunday was celebrated with a cake dance held in the main public place. A large fruit cake called a 'prioncam' cake (from 'princeam', meaning capering), was baked and decorated with heraldic beasts and birds. After plenty of drinking and dancing, one of the lads would lead the prettiest girl to the cake and place it in her hands, so crowning her Queen of the Feast. She would then divide it amongst the guests.

Easter celebrations are closely followed by May Day and Whitsuntide. In the Celtic calendar 1 May was called Beltane, and bright Beltane fires were lit on hill tops to welcome the return of summer. It was a time of elaborate festivities throughout the land, when houses were decorated with greenery, garlands were carried from house to house and the awakening earth was greeted with dancing and singing. The traditional dancing around a maypole derives from an ancient fertility rite associated with the beginning of summer. Special foods for May Day included custards, cheesecakes, Beltane oatcakes, frumenty (see page 128), syllabub, sweet cakes and hasty puddings made with flour or oatmeal and milk.

May Day festivities are all pagan in origin, but the rest of the month of May has always had several Christian festivities. Ascension Day, Whitsun and Rogation Day usually fall in May, depending on the date of Easter. Religious celebrations have gradually given place to such secular occasions as fairs, regattas and the opening of the cricket season.

Whitsun is the third most important Christian festival after Christmas and Easter. It falls seven weeks after Easter Sunday and celebrates the 'descent of the tongues of fire' and the gift of the holy spirit to Jesus's disciples at Pentecost. According to a fourteenth-century verse:

This day Whitsun day is cald
For wisdom and wit sevenfold
Was goven to the apostles on this day.

It is also thought that the name Whitsun may

derive from the white robes that were always worn for baptism.

The main event of the Whitsun festivities in most parts of Britain was the 'Church Ale'. The Ale was a parish feast rather like the Love Feasts or Agapae of the early church, when the congregation met and feasted after receiving holy communion together. The wealthier members of the church brought enough food for the poor as well as for themselves, and they ate and drank together to increase the bond of mutual love. After the feast there were often games, sports, morris dancing and drinking. The feast later became a specifically Methodist occasion, when up to 1500 people would eat together, sing hymns, give testimony and hear sermons. The meal included bread and a Love Feast cake, accompanied by water drunk from a large symbolic, two-handled communal cup passed around the entire company. From the Church Ale developed the fairs, revels and games that became the traditional activities for Whit Sunday and Monday. Around the country fairs were (and in some places still are) held with entertainments, competitions and stalls selling fancy goods that were unavailable at other times, and often special cakes, cheesecakes or sweets that were particular to each area.

May and June were busy months for farmers. Haymaking and sheep-shearing coincided with the time of year when cows were producing their maximum yield of milk.

Some of the milk was turned into the usual supply of butter, cheeses, cream cheese, curds, cream and clotted cream, and the surplus was used to make custards, cheesecakes and junkets. Junket was very popular as a festive sweet dish from the middle ages to the eighteenth century. It was served on holidays, and on feast and fair days, often called 'junket days'. The name comes from *junci*, the name of the wild rushes on which the curds were left to drain before being served.

Other popular dishes made with milk, and also closely associated with sheep-shearing and the hay harvest, were fools made with custard and fresh fruit, blancmanges flavoured with almonds, rose water or spices and creamy rice puddings. Farmers would employ extra workers to help with the haymaking and sheep-shearing, and their wives would lay on an evening meal in the farmhouse kitchen to feed all the extra mouths. Large pots of stew or huge roast joints or baked hams would be followed by rice pudding or boiled suet puddings made with figs or other dried fruit and spices. After long hours out in the fields everyone needed a hearty meal, and the communal suppers were a way of thanking the workers for their efforts of the day and an excuse for celebrating and merry-making in the evenings. The farmers were glad of the extra help and the itinerant workers were glad of the pay and the large helpings of good food.

Pea Soup

SERVES 5–6

*1 pint/2½ cups/600ml dried
    split peas*
2 onions, peeled and chopped
2 carrots, peeled and chopped
2 turnips, peeled and chopped
2 celery stalks, cut into chunks
4 or 5 cloves
*3 pints/7½ cups/1.7 litres
    ham or bacon stock
    (bouillon)*
½ pint/1¼ cups/300ml milk
*1 tsp dried mint or 2 tsp finely
    chopped fresh mint*
1 dsp moist brown sugar
pinch mustard powder
2oz/4 tbsp/50g butter
*salt and freshly ground black
    pepper*

Pea soup was traditionally made for the Monday before Lent, sometimes known as Peasen or Paisen Monday. There is a story of a farmer of Lower St Columb in Cornwall who hated pea soup so much that he would do almost anything to avoid eating it. He set off from home one Paisen Monday morning telling his wife that he was going to spend the day with a friend and would not be back for dinner. He returned two or three hours later in a very black mood since, at every house in the village, he had been invited to taste the delicious pea soup.

METHOD

Soak the split peas overnight.

Drain and place in a large saucepan with the onions, carrots, turnips, celery, cloves and stock (bouillon).

Bring to the boil and simmer for 2½–3 hours.

Work through a sieve, or put through a blender or food processor and return to the pan with the milk, mint, sugar and mustard.

Adjust the seasoning to taste and simmer for a further 15 minutes. Just before serving stir in the butter.

Lenten Kail

SERVES 4

*1lb/450g spring greens or
    green vegetables*
water
2 tbsp oatmeal
*5fl oz/½ cup + 2 tbsp/150ml
    single (coffee) cream*
*salt and freshly ground black
    pepper*

Meat and eggs were forbidden during Lent, and fish was not always readily available except for the wealthy and those living near the sea or a river. Stocks of food were often sparse during the last harsh weeks of winter and so root vegetables and spring greens formed the basis of most ordinary people's diet, with the addition of barley, oats or wheat for extra sustenance. This Scottish soup makes good use of the plentiful supply of winter and spring greens and makes a tasty and nourishing dish. Any mixture of green vegetables can be used instead of just spring greens – spinach, brussel tops, cabbage, etc.

METHOD

Put the greens into a large saucepan. Add just enough water to barely cover and bring to the boil. Simmer until tender (about 20 minutes). Drain off 10fl oz/1¼ cups/275ml of the liquid and discard. Work the rest of the liquid and the cooked cabbage through a sieve or put through a blender or food processor to form a purée and then return to the pan.

Mix the oatmeal with a little of the soup to a smooth paste, add to the pan, and stir well. Season to taste. Bring back to the boil and simmer for 15 minutes. Just before serving, stir in the cream.

Pancakes

Pancakes are cooked for Shrove Tuesday, the day before Lent begins, and were originally made to use up spare stocks of eggs and animal fat before the period of fasting began.

One of the many superstitions associated with the making and eating of pancakes was the belief, in some areas, that the first three pancakes cooked were sacred. These were marked with a cross, sprinkled with salt to ward off evil, and set aside. In the Midlands the first pancake was often given to the chickens to ensure that they laid well throughout the year.

In the north of England pancake parties were held each year on Shrove Tuesday until the 1940s. Everyone had to eat his or her pancake before the next one was ready in the pan, and there was great hilarity as others tried to slow them down by snipping the pancake from the fork with scissors.

There are so many different recipes from around Britain that it was very hard to choose which to include. Here are two very different ones: the first uses cream, and the second is a suet mixture that gives a fritter-like pancake.

Westmorland Cream Pancakes

MAKES 8 PANCAKES

1 tsp bicarbonate of soda
1 tsp cream of tartar
½ pint/1¼ cups/300ml
  single (light) cream
½ pint/1¼ cups/300ml milk
8oz/2 cups/225g plain (cake)
  flour
pinch of salt
1oz/2 tbsp/25g lard or oil for
  frying

This mixture makes a really light and fluffy pancake. Since testing it for this book I have decided it is so delicious that I shall use it again in future years instead of the more conventional recipe that simply mixes flour with egg and milk.

METHOD

Dissolve the bicarbonate of soda and the cream of tartar in the cream. Add the milk and mix well.

Sift the flour and salt into a medium-sized bowl. Make a hollow in the middle and add a little of the cream and milk mixture at a time, mixing with a wooden spoon to give a smooth batter. Beat hard for 1 minute. Leave to stand for 15 minutes.

Heat a heavy frying pan (skillet) to a steady, moderate heat. Grease with a little lard or oil. Pour one ladleful of batter into the pan and move the pan around to spread the batter evenly. Cook gently until the underside is golden. Toss and cook the other side.

Serve immediately with syrup, maple syrup, lemon or orange juice and sugar, or the following almond and apple filling.

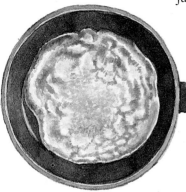

Irish Sweet Almond Filling

FILLS 4 PANCAKES

1¹/₂oz/5 tbsp/40g blanched ground almonds
1oz/2 tbsp/25g caster sugar
grated rind and juice of 3 lemons
2 medium eating apples, peeled, cored and diced
¹/₂oz/2 tbsp/15g arrowroot

In Ireland girl students were usually allowed the afternoon off school to make their pancake batter, and in the evening the young people would sit round the fire cooking pancakes. If you tossed the pancake successfully it meant that you would be married within the year.

METHOD

Mix together the almonds, sugar, lemon rind and apple.

In a small pan mix the arrowroot with a little lemon juice, then add the rest of the juice and bring to the boil, stirring all the time. Simmer for 2–3 minutes.

Pour a little of the lemon sauce into the apple mixture and mix well together. Put the remaining sauce into a sauceboat or jug.

Spread each pancake with the filling, roll up, sprinkle with sugar and serve hot with the sauce.

Gloucester Suet Pancakes

MAKES 10 PANCAKES

3oz/6 tbsp/75g finely shredded suet

These are almost like fritters and are delicious served with plenty of syrup or maple syrup, jam or lemon juice and brown sugar, or as a savoury with fried bacon and eggs.

*6oz/1½ cups/175g plain
(cake) flour plus extra for
flouring the board
1 tsp baking powder
pinch of salt
2 eggs
2 tbsp milk
lard or oil for frying*

METHOD

Mix together the suet, flour, baking powder and salt. Beat the eggs and milk together and add to the flour mixture. Mix to a stiff dough.

Place the dough on a floured board and roll out to a thickness of ½ inch/1cm. Do not roll it any thinner or the pancakes will lose their substance when you cook them.

Using a 2 inch/5cm cutter, cut the dough into 10 rounds.

Heat ¼ inch/0.5cm oil or lard in a heavy frying pan (skillet) to a low even heat. Cook the pancakes until golden on one side, then turn and brown the other side. Serve immediately.

Tatie Hash

SERVES 4

*1lb/450g loin or breast of
lamb
6oz/1 cup/175g black
pudding, thinly sliced
2 large onions, peeled and
sliced
3–4 carrots, peeled and thinly
sliced
3lb/1.35kg potatoes, thinly
sliced
1 tsp dried mixed herbs
salt and freshly ground black
pepper
½ pint/1¼ cups/300ml stock
(bouillon)*

In some northern counties of England this was a favourite dish for Ash Wednesday, so giving rise to confusion about the origins of the day's name (the true reason derives from the custom of the early Christian church of sprinkling ashes on the heads of those who confessed their sins). Meat was added later as rules of abstinence slackened over the years. The recipe uses uncooked mutton or lamb but left-over cooked meat would also be suitable.

METHOD

Preheat the oven to gas 5/190°C/375°F.

Prepare the meat by cutting into small pieces and discarding any fat or gristle.

Grease a deep pie dish. Arrange layers of lamb, black pudding and vegetables, adding a sprinkling of herbs, salt and pepper between each layer. Make the last layer of potatoes.

Pour over the stock (bouillon). Cover and cook for 1 hour. Remove the lid or cover and cook for a further hour to allow the potatoes to brown.

Old English Fish Pie

SERVES 4

FOR THE CRUST

Shortcrust pastry made with 8oz/2 cups/225g plain (cake) flour (see page 132)

FOR THE FILLING

1lb/450g cod fillets, steamed and flaked, and any skin and bones discarded

2 large onions, peeled and sliced

4 eggs, hard-boiled and sliced

2oz/1 cup/50g button mushrooms, cleaned and sliced

2 tbsp chopped fresh parsley

2–3 cloves

salt and freshly ground black pepper

2 tsp mustard powder

1–2 tsp anchovy essence

2–3 tbsp hot water

1 egg, beaten

Pies date back to the eleventh or twelfth century when meats generally, and birds in particular, were served 'in their coffins'. Over the centuries all sorts of fish pies were developed for Lent, some of them very elaborate with fancy raised crusts, and filled with almost any fish available. Many contained chopped or sliced hard-boiled eggs, going against earlier Lenten prohibitions.

The original recipe for this fish pie uses mushroom ketchup (catsup) but this is sometimes difficult to find, so I have substituted fresh mushrooms instead. If mushroom ketchup (catsup) is used, mix it with the anchovy essence and hot water before pouring over the contents of the dish.

METHOD

First make the pastry as on page 132 and chill for at least 15 minutes. Preheat the oven to gas 4/180°C/350°F. Grease an ovenproof pie dish.

On a floured board roll out the pastry to ½ inch/1cm thick to fit the pie dish. Keep any trimmings to use as crosses on hot cross buns. Place in the dish layers of fish, onions, eggs and sliced mushrooms, sprinkling a little parsley, the cloves, salt, pepper and mustard powder between the layers. The dish should be about three-quarters full.

Mix the anchovy essence with the hot water and pour over. Dot the top with little knobs of butter and cover with the pastry lid. Trim the edges and press well down on to the rim of the dish. Brush with beaten egg and make a small hole in the middle.

Bake for 1 hour just below the middle of the oven. If the pastry begins to brown too quickly, cover with several layers of folded greaseproof paper.

Herb Pudding

SERVES 4

1lb/450g green vegetables (spring greens, cabbage, Brussels sprouts, cauliflower, broccoli, watercress, lettuce,

This Lent recipe makes excellent use of winter root vegetables and early spring greens. In the past the savoury pudding was made with whatever vegetables and herbs were available, and such things as leeks, young dandelion leaves, gooseberry or blackcurrant leaves were added to give a good strong flavour that helped make up for the lack of meat. The addition of barley or oatmeal made it a very

spinach, young nettle
leaves, young dandelion
leaves etc.)
2–3 small turnips, carrots,
beats or other root vegetable
2 small leeks, washed,
trimmed and cut into thin
slices
1 tbsp chopped fresh mixed
herbs (sage, thyme,
marjoram, parsley etc.) or
2 tsp dried mixed herbs
2oz/2 tbsp/50g barley or
oatmeal
salt and freshly ground black
pepper
2 eggs, beaten

nourishing dish that was eaten as a meal in itself. Today it makes a really delicious accompaniment to meat dishes and the barley or oatmeal gives it a good, nutty flavour.

The mixture may also be cooked in a pastry crust.

METHOD

Wash and slice or chop the vegetables and mix together with the leeks, herbs and barley or oatmeal.

Place the mixture in a pudding bowl and cover with foil, or greaseproof paper and a linen cloth. Tie a piece of string tightly round the rim and steam for approximately two hours until the barley is soft.

Preheat the oven to Gas 4/180°C/350°F.

Turn the mixture from the pudding bowl into a mixing bowl and add the beaten egg and seasoning. Turn into an ovenproof pie dish or casserole and bake for 30 minutes until just brown and slightly crispy on top.

Cawl

SERVES 8–10

2oz/4 tbsp/50g butter
2lb/900g Welsh lamb, cut
into chunks
1lb/450g potatoes, peeled and
cut into chunks
2 large parsnips, peeled and
sliced
3 large carrots, peeled and
sliced
1 turnip, peeled and diced
2 medium onions, roughly
chopped
1 tsp dried thyme
1 or 2 cloves
2 large leeks, trimmed,
washed and cut into 1 inch/
2.5cm pieces
1oz/¼ cup/25g plain (cake)
flour or oatmeal
salt and freshly ground black
pepper
2 tbsp chopped fresh parsley

This broth, made with lamb and leeks is a national dish in Wales, served on festive occasions and St David's Day (1 March).

The leek is one of the Welsh national emblems (the other is the daffodil) and is associated with St David, who is said to have 'fed upon the leeks that he gathered in the fields'.

This broth used to be served as two courses – the liquid soup first, followed by the meat and vegetables. Today it is normally served as one dish, often in a wooden bowl, and eaten with a wooden spoon.

METHOD

Melt the butter in a large pan and brown the meat. Cover with cold water, bring to simmering point and simmer for about 1 hour, skimming off any scum as it rises.

Add the potatoes, parsnips, carrots, turnip, onion, thyme and cloves and simmer for about 30 minutes. Mix the flour or oatmeal with a little cold water and add to the pan. Stir well and leave to simmer for a further 15 minutes.

Add the leeks, season to taste and cook for 10–15 minutes more. Just before serving stir in the parsley.

Baked Whiting

SERVES 2

4oz/4–5 slices/100g stale, crustless white or brown bread

water or milk

1 medium onion, peeled and finely chopped

2oz/4 tbsp/50g butter

salt and freshly ground black pepper

2 tbsp chopped fresh parsley

pinch of dried sage

pinch of mace

2 egg yolks

1 whiting – gutted and cleaned

Fish was an excellent source of nourishment during Lent, for those who could afford it and who had access to a supply. In large manor houses vast quantities of fish were imported at the beginning of Lent, and throughout the season, barrels of extra supplies of white and red pickled herrings were brought in. Sixteenth-century records from a large manor house near Chelmsford in Essex show that for lunch one day during Lent the servants and five visitors shared half a ling (a little like a large cod), half a haberdine (a dried salt cod), two mudfish, thirty-six white herring, twenty-six red herring, four cakes of butter and four eggs. The records also show that they did not eat any supper that night!

This London recipe for baked whiting is from the 1930s.

METHOD

Preheat the oven to gas 5/190°C/375°F.

Soak the bread in water or milk, then squeeze out. Put into a small bowl and break up with a fork or wooden spoon.

In a small pan fry the onion in a little of the butter until soft but not brown. Add the remaining butter and allow to melt over a low heat.

Add the bread, salt and pepper, parsley, sage and mace. Mix well and stir over a low heat until heated through. Add the egg yolks and beat well together.

Stuff the fish rather full and sew up or bind with string to hold in shape. Rub the fish with a little melted butter, sprinkle with salt and pepper and place in an ovenproof dish. Bake for 30–35 minutes.

Roast Loin of Veal

SERVES 4

FOR THE STUFFING

2oz/¹/₂ cup/50g ham or lean
  bacon
4oz/¹/₂ cup/100g suet
6oz/3 cups/175g breadcrumbs
grated rind of half a lemon
1 tbsp chopped fresh parsley
1 tsp dried sweet herbs
  (marjoram, thyme, basil)
salt and freshly ground black
  pepper
pinch of cayenne pepper
pinch of ground mace
2 eggs, beaten
2lb/900g piece of loin of veal
  (ask the butcher to cut into
  one side of the meat to make
  a pocket for the stuffing)
plain (cake) flour for
  dredging

After attending church on Mothering Sunday, the family would share a festive meal of roast veal or pork, or, for the less well-off, bacon and peas. The main course was often followed by an egg custard or a Mothering Sunday pudding made with raisins and figs. These foods were permitted because this weekend in Lent was a recognized relaxation from fasting, and the Sunday was also known as Refreshment or Refection Sunday. The roast veal was often served with a sauce made with eggs and dried fish.

METHOD

Preheat the oven to gas 5/190°C/375°F.

Mix all the ingredients for the stuffing together until evenly blended. Carefully open up the pocket in the meat and gradually push the stuffing inside. Secure the opening with skewers or stitch with strong thread.

Dredge the joint with plain (cake) flour. Place a few knobs of butter over the top and roast for 2 hours (25 minutes per lb + 25 minutes).

Simnel Cake

**MAKES 1 × 2lb/900g
ROUND CAKE**

*6oz/1½ cups/175g plain
(cake) flour*

1 tsp baking powder

pinch of salt

1 tsp mixed spice

*5oz/½ cup + 2 tbsp/150g
butter or margarine,
softened*

*5oz/½ cup + 2 tbsp/150g
moist brown sugar*

3–4 eggs

*12oz/3 cups/350g mixed
dried fruit (currants,
sultanas, raisins, mixed
peel)*

*2oz/4 tbsp/50g glacé cherries,
halved*

finely grated rind of one lemon

2 tbsp milk

apricot jam or jelly

FOR THE ALMOND PASTE

*6oz/1½ cups/175g ground
almonds*

*5oz/½ cup + 2 tbsp/150g
icing (confectioners') sugar*

*5oz/½ cup + 2 tbsp/150g
caster sugar*

*½ tsp almond essence
(extract)*

1 tsp lemon juice

1 egg, beaten

or 1lb ready-made paste.

Simnel cakes, also called Lenten cakes, were originally made for Mothering Sunday but today are more often eaten at Easter. 'Simnel' probably derives from the Latin *simila*, meaning fine flour, and the cake may date back to the time of the Roman occupation. The name may also have Anglo-Saxon origins, from *symel* or *symbel*, meaning a feast. The early cakes in some areas were thin, crisp wafers rather than the fruit cake we know today, and were stamped with the figure of either the Virgin Mary or Christ. The eleven balls of marzipan that are traditionally placed around the top represent eleven of the twelve apostles (Judas is excluded).

It was the custom for children working away from home to return to the family on Mothering Sunday in order to go to the mother church to make Lenten offerings. They would bring with them simnel cake as a gift for their mother.

This recipe was sent to me by Mrs J M Train of Teignmouth, Devon.

METHOD

First make the almond paste. Put the dry ingredients into a bowl and mix well. Add the almond essence and lemon juice and enough beaten egg to form a stiff paste. Wrap in foil or cling-film until required.

Grease and line a 2lb/900g round cake tin with a double layer of greaseproof paper. Preheat the oven to Gas 2/150°C/300°F.

Mix together the flour, baking powder, salt and mixed spice.

Beat the butter or margarine with the sugar until light and fluffy. Add the eggs, one at a time, adding 2 tbsp of the flour mixture with each egg and beating well after each addition. Stir in the remaining flour mixture, the dried fruit, lemon rind and milk.

Turn half of the mixture into the prepared tin. Divide the almond paste into three portions. Roll out one portion to a circle just smaller than the diameter of the tin. Place this on top of the mixture in the tin, then add the rest of the cake mixture on top.

Bake for approximately 2½ hours, until a warm skewer comes out clean. Remove from the oven and leave to cool in the tin for 10 minutes before turning out on to a wire rack to cool completely.

Roll out the second portion of almond paste to a circle to fit the top of the cake. Brush the top of the cake with apricot jam or jelly and place the circle of almond paste on top. Press down lightly with a rolling pin. Make the remaining almond paste into eleven little balls and arrange these around the top edge of the cake, sticking them in place with a little apricot jam or jelly. Place the whole cake under a low grill (broiler) for about 3 minutes to just brown the top.

To serve, arrange a few fresh flowers on the top and wrap the sides of the cake with a wide, primrose-yellow satin ribbon.

Fig Pie

SERVES 8

*rich shortcrust pastry made
  with 8oz/2 cups/225g plain
  (cake) flour (see page 132)*
*1lb 4oz/3 cups/550g dried
  figs, each one cut in half*
2 tbsp water
4 tsp cornflower (cornstarch)
1 tsp mixed spice
4oz/1 cup/100g currants
1 tbsp black treacle (molasses)

Until the 1930s, Palm Sunday (the sixth Sunday in Lent) was widely known in many regions of Britain as Fig Sunday, and it was a day when everybody ate figs. In most regions nearly every household would eat fig or fag pudding or pie on Palm Sunday and offer it to visitors, while children were often given little bags of figs in the morning to remind them what day it was.

This pie can be made as an open or covered pie with a pastry lid placed over the figs before baking. The recipe given here is for an open pie, and a covered pie will obviously need more pastry.

METHOD

First make the pastry as on page 132 and chill for at least 15 minutes or until needed.

Preheat the oven to gas 5/190°C/375°F. Grease a 9 inch/23cm pie or flan dish.

On a floured surface roll out the pastry to a thickness of ⅜ inch/1cm and line the prepared pie dish. Cut strips from the spare pastry about ¾ inch/2cm wide. Brush one side of the strips with milk and press firmly against the first layer of pastry round the inner edge of the dish to make a double edging. Make a pattern around this edge with a knife blade or fork prongs.

Put the figs in a pan with just enough water to cover them. Stew gently until tender.

Mix the cornflour (cornstarch) with 2 tbsp cold water and add to the pan. Stir until the juice thickens. Stir in the treacle (molasses), spice and currants and mix well so that all the ingredients are evenly distributed.

Pour the mixture into the prepared pastry case and level with a palette knife. Bake for 30 minutes until the pastry is golden and the figs nicely browned.

Serve with custard or cream.

Good Friday Fish Pie

SERVES 4

1lb/450g cod or haddock
*   fillets*
1 pint/2½ cups/600ml milk
salt and freshly ground black
*   pepper*
1½oz/3 tbsp/40g butter
1½oz/6 tbsp/40g plain
*   (cake) flour*
3 tbsp chopped fresh parsley
2lb/900g potatoes
a little milk or cream
1–2 oz/2–4 tbsp/25–50g
*   butter*
4oz/1½ cups/100g grated
*   cheese*

In Cornwall, Good Friday was the day when everybody went down to the Helford River, once famous for its oysters, to gather limpets (also known as fritters), cockles and winkles. These were collected in sacks and taken home to be eaten for supper.

In most parts of Britain in recent years, the most popular fish dish for Good Friday has been cod or haddock, either served in a pie with a pastry or potato topping, or with parsley sauce and young spring peas.

METHOD

Preheat the oven to gas 5/190°C/375°F.

Place the fish in an ovenproof dish and pour over the milk. Sprinkle with a little salt and pepper and bake for 15 minutes until the fish flakes easily.

Strain the milk from the fish and reserve for the sauce. Flake the fish and remove any skin and bones. Put the flaked fish back into the dish.

Melt the butter in a medium-sized saucepan, add the flour and mix well. Let the mixture bubble gently for 2 minutes, stirring all the time. Remove from the heat and gradually add the milk stock, the parsley and salt and pepper to taste. Place back on the heat and bring to the boil, stirring constantly until the sauce thickens. Pour over the fish.

Meanwhile boil the potatoes in salted water for about 20 minutes. When cooked, drain and mash with a little milk or cream, butter and pepper. Spread the potato over the fish, smooth the top and mark with the prongs of a fork. Sprinkle the grated cheese over the top and bake for 20–25 minutes until the cheese is just turning golden and bubbly.

Serve with fresh peas either mixed in with the fish or as an accompaniment.

Salt Beef and Cabbage

SERVES 4–5

1¼lb/550g salt beef
1lb/450g cabbage
3oz/6 tbsp/75g butter
5 or 6 juniper berries
freshly ground black pepper

This is really the forerunner of what we know today as 'bubble and squeak'. It was popular in Britain as far back as the sixteenth century, when recipes spoke of 'long wortes' (vegetables), and especially cabbage, with 'powdred beef' – meat sprinkled with salt to preserve it. Later versions used cold cooked meat, and our modern recipes use no meat at all, but mix potatoes with the cabbage. The correct name for this is 'colcannon', a favourite Irish and Scottish dish that is cooked for Hallowe'en (see page 91).

This dish of salt beef (what the Irish call corned beef) was cooked in Ireland on Easter Sunday by those who could not afford or had no access to the traditional piece of roast veal or spring lamb or kid.

METHOD

Soak the meat overnight to remove some of the salt. Boil it in fresh water for 45 minutes until tender. Leave to cool in the water as this will improve the flavour. When cold remove from the water and slice.

Heat the oven to gas 2/150°C/200°F. Warm a serving dish.

Boil the cabbage in a little lightly salted water until just tender. Drain thoroughly and chop.

Melt the butter in a frying pan (skillet) and add the juniper berries. Add the slices of meat and season with black pepper. Cook gently until browned.

Remove the meat from the pan and keep warm in the oven. Place the cabbage in the frying pan (skillet) and fry for a few minutes.

Lay the cabbage in the centre of the warmed serving dish and arrange the slices of meat around it. Serve immediately.

Hare Pie

SERVES 5–6

rough puff pastry made with
8oz/2 cups/225g plain
(cake) flour (see page 133)
forcemeat balls (see page 54)
1 hare, boned and cut up
5–6 slices of ham, diced
3–4 hard-boiled eggs, sliced

The hare was sacred to Eastre, the Saxon goddess of spring. The earliest records describe ritual hunts for hares to sacrifice in her honour. At Hallaton in Leicestershire the villagers still meet together on Easter Monday for the annual Hare Pie Scramble, which is no doubt a more recent version of the pagan practice. The Hallaton custom, first recorded in 1668, is connected with a piece of land that at some unknown date was bequeathed to successive rectors, on condition that each in his turn should provide at Easter

1 medium onion, thinly sliced
salt and freshly ground black
*   pepper*
a pinch of mace
1 tsp mixed herbs
½ pint/1¼ cups/300ml
*   gravy or stock (bouillon)*

every year two hare pies, a quantity of ale and two dozen penny loaves to be scrambled for. Each year the pies are still made in the rectory kitchen, but nowadays they contain beef, as hare is more difficult to obtain.

METHOD

Make the pastry as on page 133 and chill for at least 15 minutes.

Preheat the oven to gas 7/220°C/425°F. Grease a large pie dish.

Make the forcemeat balls by mixing all the ingredients together and then shaping into little balls. Put the hare, ham, forcemeat balls, sliced eggs and onion in layers in the dish, adding a little seasoning to each layer. Add the gravy or stock.

On a floured board, roll out the pastry to make a lid and use to cover the pie. Bake for 15 minutes then reduce the heat to gas 4/180°C/350°F and bake for a further 1¼–1½ hours. If the pastry becomes too brown cover it with greaseproof paper.

Easterledge Pudding

SERVES 4

1lb/450g young bistorts or
*   nettle tops, finely chopped*
1 large onion, finely chopped
4oz/½ cup/100g barley
½ tsp salt
1 egg, beaten
1oz/2 tbsp/25g butter
freshly ground black pepper
oil or fat (shortening) for
*   frying*

This rather strange name is thought to come from 'astrologia', an earlier name for bistorts, the main ingredient for this Easter savoury. It is likely that astrologia developed into Easter-logia and thus became associated with the celebrations of Easter. Bistort is also known as Passion Dock, and as the recipe is sometimes called Passion Dock Pudding it has gained obvious associations with Christ's passion.

Although the pudding is not commonly known today, it is still made in some areas of northern England. It would probably have been eaten with eggs and bacon, or fried potatoes and chopped hard-boiled eggs, or, in earlier days, as a starter course on its own. Until potatoes became a standard part of our diet, a plain or savoury pudding was often served as a filler course at the beginning of the meal to fill people up before the meat course.

METHOD

Mix together the chopped greens, onion, barley and salt. Tie inside a pudding bag or put into a pudding bowl and cover with greaseproof paper and a linen cloth. Boil or steam for 2 hours.

Remove from the bag or bowl and turn into a large mixing bowl. Add the egg, butter and pepper to taste and mix well. Shape into a flat cake and fry in oil or fat (shortening) until brown on both sides.

Serve immediately.

Hot Cross Buns

MAKES 16–18

*1lb/4 cups/450g plain (cake)
    flour, warmed*

½ tsp salt

*2oz/4 tbsp/50g margarine, or
    margarine and lard mixed*

4 tsp fresh yeast

4oz/½ cup/100g sugar

1 tsp mixed spice or cinnamon

1–2 eggs

*8–10 fl oz/1–1¼ cups/225–
    300ml milk, warmed*

2oz/⅓ cup/50g currants

*pastry trimmings to make the
    crosses*

beaten egg and water to glaze

The Christian tradition of baking special cakes has its precursors in several ancient cultures. The Aztecs in Mexico, the Egyptians, the Greeks and the Romans all made a round cake or bun and divided it with a cross into the four quarters of the moon to honour their various gods and goddesses. The mark of the cross – probably also intended to ward off the evil spirits that might stop the bread dough from rising – was adopted by the Christian church to represent Christ's cross.

Early bakers used a wooden 'docker' to mark the cross on each bun, but the action of bringing this down on top of the risen dough tended to knock all the air out, and the proving process had to start again. So the docker was later replaced by batter or rice paper.

METHOD

Mix the salt with the warmed flour. Rub or cut in the fat (shortening).

Cream the yeast with 1 tsp of the sugar, then mix with the rest of the sugar, spice and eggs. Add to the flour with enough warmed milk to make a soft, light dough. Beat well. Cover with a damp cloth and put in a warm place to rise for about 1 hour.

Grease two baking trays.

When the dough is well risen mix in the currants with a fork. The dough will be wet and sticky. Using two spoons, place 16–18 rounds of dough on the prepared trays, leaving space between. Leave in a warm place for a further 15 minutes to rise.

Meanwhile heat the oven to gas 7/220°C/425°F.

Cut strips of thin pastry to form crosses. Brush the tops of the buns with beaten egg and water and place a cross on each. Bake 15–20 minutes until nicely browned. Remove from the oven and lift on to a wire rack to cool.

Hertfordshire Easter Pies

MAKES 15 TARTS

*Rich shortcrust pastry made
with 8oz/2 cups/225g plain
(cake) flour (see page 132)*
8oz/1 cup/225g caster sugar
2oz/4 tbsp/50g butter
*grated rind of 2 lemons and
the juice of 3*
*1oz/¼ cup/25g ground
almonds*
3 eggs, beaten
*1 cream cracker biscuit,
crumbled*

These little pies are a typical example of early English cheesecakes. Hertfordshire is said to have excelled in the making of cheesecakes; the historian Reginald Hine likened eating a Hitchin cheesecake to 'a progress through paradise'. There are records of a Hertfordshire Easter cheesecake that was actually made with cheese, but this one with lemon curd filling was more common.

METHOD

Make the pastry as on page 132 and chill for at least 15 minutes.

Preheat the oven to gas 4/180°C/350°F. Grease 15 patty tins.

On a floured board roll out the pastry to a thickness of approximately ¼ inch/0.5cm. Using a 2½ inch/7cm cutter, cut 15 rounds and use to line the prepared patty tins.

Put all the ingredients for the filling into a bowl over a pan of boiling water (or a double saucepan). Cook, stirring all the time, until thick. This will take 10–15 minutes. Do not allow to boil.

Spoon the filling into the pastry cases and bake for 12–15 minutes until the pastry is golden and the filling firm to the touch. Remove from the oven and allow to cool for 15 minutes in the tins before lifting out on to a wire rack to cool completely.

Kentish Pudding Pies

MAKES 24 PIES

*shortcrust pastry made with
8oz/2 cups/225g plain
(cake) flour (see page 132)*
1 pint/2½ cups/600ml milk
3 strips of lemon rind
*3oz/just under ½ cup/75g
ground rice*
pinch of salt
2oz/4 tbsp/50g butter
3oz/6 tbsp/75g sugar
2 eggs
2oz/⅓ cup/50g currants

Like egg custards these pies were made to use up some of the spare eggs laid during Lent. They were eaten at Easter with cherry beer – a strong ale with cherry juice added. There are several different recipes from around Kent. This one comes from Folkstone and makes a very delicate, light tart.

METHOD

Make the pastry as on page 132 and chill for at least 15 minutes.

Preheat the oven to gas 4/180°C/350°F. Grease 24 patty tins.

On a floured board roll out the pastry to a thickness of approximately ¼ inch/0.5 cm, and cut rounds using a 2½ inch/ 7 cm cutter. Use these to line the patty tins.

Boil ¾ of the milk with the lemon rind for a few minutes. Remove the lemon rind.

Mix together the ground rice, salt and the remaining milk, taking care that no lumps form. Add to the boiling milk and stir thoroughly. Bring to the boil and simmer gently, stirring continuously for 5–6 minutes.

Add the butter and sugar and beat well, then add the eggs, one at a time, beating hard after the addition of each egg. Stir in the currants.

Divide the mixture between the patty cases and bake for 12–15 minutes until the pastry is golden and the filling is well puffed up and firm.

Remove from the oven and allow to cool in the tins for at least 15 minutes before lifting out.

Custard Tart

SERVES 6–8

shortcrust pastry made with 8oz/2 cups/225g plain (cake) flour (see page 132)

3 eggs

¾ pint/just over 1¾ cups/ 450ml milk

2 tbsp double (whipping) cream

1–2 tbsp sugar, to taste

grated nutmeg

Doris Ling from Suffolk wrote to me that when she was a child, 'Never an Easter Sunday passed without a very large egg custard with a pastry bottom, and a rhubarb pie.' In Oxfordshire the two days of the Easter weekend, were known as Egg Saturday and Egg Sunday. In Yorkshire the prevailing wind was often called 'custard wind'. Custards and cheesecakes were regularly made for Eastertide in East Anglia, Hertfordshire, Warwickshire and Kent. In Scotland pancakes were sometimes cooked to use some of the extra eggs.

METHOD

Make the pastry as on page 132 and chill for at least 15 minutes.

Preheat the oven to gas 6/200°C/400°F. Grease an 8 inch/20 cm pie or flan dish.

On a floured board roll out the pastry and use to line the dish. Prick the base all over and bake blind for 5 minutes just to set the pastry.

Beat the eggs with the milk, cream and sugar. Pour into the pastry case and sprinkle the nutmeg over the top.

Reduce the oven temperature to gas 4/180°C/350°F and bake the pie for 1¼ hours until the custard is set.

Spiced Currant Dumplings

MAKES 10 DUMPLINGS

4oz/1 cup/100g plain (cake)
*   flour*
¹/₂ tsp baking powder
4oz/1 cup/100g fresh
*   breadcrumbs*
4oz/1 cup/100g shredded suet
4oz/²/₃ cup/100g currants
2oz/4 tbsp/50g sugar
1 tsp grated nutmeg
¹/₂ tsp mixed spice
2 eggs, beaten
a little milk, if necessary

FOR THE SAUCE

1¹/₂oz/3 tbsp/40g butter
1¹/₂oz/6 tbsp/40g plain
*   (cake) flour*
1 pint/2¹/₂ cups/600ml milk
grated rind and juice of
1 lemon
4oz/¹/₂ cup/100g sugar

These dumplings were popular for Easter in the Cambridge area. Dumplings were originally made with bread dough taken from the weekly batch. The dough was formed into little balls and cooked in the same pot as the boiled beef that they traditionally accompany, or baked separately. Suet was used later to give a more solid, heavy dough that was better boiled than baked.

METHOD

Mix all the ingredients together and, if needed, add enough milk to make a firm dough. With floured fingers, shape into 10 dumplings.

Bring a pan of water to the boil and carefully drop the dumplings into it. Boil for 10 minutes, lift out with a slotted spoon and immediately tear each one slightly apart with two forks to let the steam out, or they will be sad and heavy in the middle. Serve hot with lemon sauce.

Melt the butter in a saucepan. Stir in the flour and allow to bubble for 2–3 minutes on a gentle heat, stirring all the time.

Remove from the heat and gradually add the milk, then the lemon rind and sugar. Return to the heat and stir continuously until the sauce thickens. Leave to cool for 2–3 minutes, then stir in the lemon juice. Serve immediately.

Easter Biscuits

MAKES 12–14

4oz/¹/₂ cup/100g butter,
*   softened*
2oz/4 tbsp/50g lard, softened
8oz/2 cups/225g plain (cake)
*   flour*
4oz/¹/₂ cup/100g sugar
8oz/1¹/₂ cups/225g currants
1oz/1 tbsp/25g mixed candied
*   peel*
¹/₂ tsp mixed spice
1 egg, beaten with 1 tbsp
*   brandy*
1 tsp lemon juice

There are recipes for these biscuits (cookies) from all over Britain. They vary very little, the main difference being that some use brandy and others do not. A West Country recipe uses mixed spice as well as cinnamon, and a 1904 recipe from Devon leaves out the spices and the brandy. This recipe was sent to me by Jenny Marsland from her guest house on the Isle of Sark in the Channel Islands. The biscuits are deliciously light and full of currants.

METHOD

Preheat the oven to gas 6/200°C/400°F. Grease a large baking tray.

Rub or cut the butter and lard into the flour to make a rather wet and sticky mixture. Stir in the sugar, currants, peel and spice.

Add the egg, brandy and lemon juice and mix with a fork to a firm dough.

Knead lightly to work the dough well together.

On a floured board roll the dough out to a thickness of approximately ½ inch/1 cm, and cut rounds about 4 inches/10 cm in diameter (or smaller if preferred).

Set on the prepared tray and bake for about 15–20 minutes until pale golden brown. Remove from the oven and leave to cool on the tray for about 15 minutes before lifting on to a wire rack to cool completely.

Saffron Cake

MAKES 1 × 9 INCH/23CM ROUND CAKE

¼ tsp saffron strands
pinch of salt
2.5 fl oz/4½ tbsp/65ml cold water
1lb/4 cups/450g plain (cake) flour
¼ tsp bicarbonate of soda
8oz/1 cup/225g margarine or butter
2oz/½ cup/50g mixed candied peel
6oz/just over 1 cup/175g sultanas
8oz/1½ cups/225g currants
6oz/¾ cup/175g sugar
2 eggs, beaten
a little milk

In Devon and Cornwall saffron cake and little saffron buns were eaten with clotted cream at Easter. Saffron is thought to have come originally from Greece and Asia Minor and is recorded as having arrived in Britain during the reign of Edward III (1327–77). Saffron-growing was established at Saffron Walden in Essex at that time but did not last long. By the beginning of the fifteenth century it had died out, and supplies were again being imported from the East. It was a very popular ingredient in medieval cookery for flavouring and colouring, and it was also believed to have healing powers.

This recipe was sent to me by Mrs Gronhaug of Boston, Lancashire.

METHOD

Put the saffron into a basin with a pinch of salt and 2.5 fl oz/4½ tbsp/65ml cold water and leave to soak overnight.

Preheat the oven to gas 4/180°C/350°F. Grease and line a 9 inch/ 23 cm round tin so that the greaseproof paper stands above the top of the tin.

Sift together the flour and bicarbonate of soda and rub or cut in the margarine or butter. Add the peel, sultanas, currants and sugar and mix well.

Stir in the beaten eggs and strained saffron water. Add enough milk to mix to a dropping consistency. Beat well and turn into the prepared tin.

Bake for 1½–2 hours until a warm skewer comes out clean. Remove from the oven and leave to cool in the tin for 10 minutes before turning on to a wire rack to cool completely.

Dorset Treacle Tart

SERVES 6

*shortcrust pastry made with
8oz/2 cups/225g plain
(cake) flour (see page 132)*
*4oz/1 cup/100g fresh
breadcrumbs*
a pinch of mixed spice
a pinch of ground ginger
2 tbsp black treacle (molasses)
*8oz/1½ cups/225g mixed
dried fruit*
*grated rind and juice of 1
lemon*
*1 large eating apple, finely
chopped*

At Wareham in Dorset a Cuckoo Fair was always held on or near 17 April, when the cuckoo normally arrived in the county. Special foods at the fairground included toffee apples and this treacle tart.

METHOD

Make the pastry as on page 132 and chill for at least 15 minutes.

Preheat the oven to gas 4/180°C/350°F. Grease an 8 inch/20 cm fluted pie dish.

On a floured board roll out two-thirds of the pastry and use to line the dish. Roll out the remaining third to form a lid and set aside.

Mix together all the ingredients for the filling and turn into the pastry case. Cover with the pastry lid and pinch the edges firmly together.

Bake for 30 minutes until golden. Serve hot or cold with plenty of cream or custard.

Hasty Pudding

SERVES 4

1 pint/2½ cups/600ml milk
1 tbsp plain (cake) flour
a pinch of salt
1 tbsp fine or medium oatmeal

Irish children used to celebrate May Day by eating this blancmange-like pudding made with milk, sugar, flour and flavourings, while adults ate bowlsful of curds, cheese and milk. Hasty pudding was also popular in England during May, when there was a plentiful supply of milk. Some recipes use oatmeal, tapioca or sago to give a more substantial pudding, and beaten egg

was sometimes added to make the mixture richer and creamier. Others use just milk, flour and sugar. Generally the pudding was eaten with cream, sugar, treacle or jam.

At midsummer in Pendine, Carmarthenshire, people went from house to house asking for milk to make a midsummer pudding – similar to Hasty pudding. Apparently the milk was given willingly and generously.

This recipe comes from Lancashire.

METHOD

Mix the flour, salt and oatmeal with ½ cup of the milk to make a thick paste. Bring the rest of the milk to the boil and mix with the paste. Stir well, return to the heat and cook, stirring all the time, until thick.

(If liked, add a beaten egg to the mixture before the hot milk.)

Burnt Cream

SERVES 4

*1 pint/2½ cups/600ml double
  (whipping) cream
2 drops vanilla essence
  (extract)
6 egg yolks
1oz/2½ tbsp/25g caster sugar*

This recipe from Cambridge University was cooked as part of the May Week celebrations. It was introduced by a fellow of Trinity College in 1879 and is also called Trinity cream or Cambridge cream. Great ceremony was always involved in the cracking of the sugary topping.

METHOD

Preheat the oven to gas 3/170°C/325°F.

Put the cream and vanilla into a double boiler or a bowl set over a pan of simmering water. Bring almost to the boil.

Beat the egg yolks and sugar together. Pour the cream on to the eggs and sugar, and whisk. Pour into a shallow dish and place in a tin of hot water so that the water comes about half way up the outside of the dish.

Bake for 30 minutes. Remove from the oven and cool in the refrigerator until solid.

Just before serving preheat the grill to high. Sprinkle the caster sugar over the cream. Place the dish on a tray of ice cubes to prevent the pudding from melting and put it under the grill (broiler) until the sugar melts and bubbles. Watch it all the time to check that the cream is not melting.

Chill again and serve.

Banbury Cakes

MAKES 14 CAKES

*flaky pastry made with 8oz/2
   cups/225g plain (cake)
   flour (see page 132)*

FOR THE FILLING

1oz/2 tbsp/25g butter, melted
*½oz/2 tbsp/15g plain (cake)
   flour*
¼ tsp grated nutmeg
4oz/⅔ cup/100g currants
1oz/1 tbsp/25g candied peel
*2oz/⅓ cup/50g soft brown
   sugar*
1 tbsp brandy
1 tbsp rum
1 tsp rosewater
beaten egg for glazing
caster sugar for dredging

Banbury cakes date back to pagan days and have always had associations with May Day celebrations. Young people would climb a hill, light a fire and bake a cake. When this had been divided up, one piece was blackened with charcoal or in the embers, and whoever got that piece was destined to be 'sacrificed' to Baal. In the seventeenth century the Puritans banned May Day festivities but the Banbury cakes survived. Then as now the cakes had a pastry crust filled with spiced fruit, while in the eighteenth century they lost their crust and became more of a spiced fruit bread with caraway seeds. Another version for the same period used saffron and sherry. Most modern recipes use flaky pastry and have a brandy or rum-flavoured filling. Whatever the recipe, the cakes should be very brittle and should always be eaten fresh and hot.

METHOD

Make the pastry as on page 132 and chill for at least 15 minutes.

Preheat the oven to gas 7/220°C/425°F. Grease two baking trays.

Mix together all the ingredients for the filling, making sure they are evenly distributed.

On a floured board roll out the pastry to a thickness of approximately ¼ inch/0.5 cm and cut into 3 inch/7.5 cm rounds. Place a good spoonful of the filling on to each round.

Dampen the edges and gather them together to enclose the filling. Press well together. Turn each cake over and roll gently into an oval shape. Brush the tops with beaten egg and make 3 cuts across the top of each.

Dust with caster sugar and place the cakes on the prepared trays. Bake for 20–25 minutes until the pastry is crisp and golden. Remove from the oven and lift carefully on to a wire rack to cool.

Helston Pudding

SERVES 5–6

½ tsp bicarbonate of soda
4 fl oz/½ cup/100ml milk
2oz/¼ cup/50g sugar
2oz/⅓ cup/50g raisins
2oz/⅓ cup/50g currants
2oz/½ cup/50g fresh
  breadcrumbs
2oz/½ cup/50g plain (cake)
  flour
pinch of salt
1 tbsp candied peel
2oz/⅓ cup/50g ground rice
2oz/½ cup/50g shredded suet
½ tsp mixed spice

St Michael is the patron saint of Helston in Cornwall, and the feast day which marks the church anniversary is held on 8 May (although St Michael's Day is celebrated nationally on 29 September). Helston celebrates with the Helston Furry Dance, when the townspeople dance through the streets from dawn to dusk, said to commemorate the day St Michael fought with the devil for possession of the town. When St Michael won everybody danced for joy in the streets.

The name of the dance varies from Furry to Floral, Flora and Faddy, names which are thought to derive from the Cornish word 'feur' meaning a fair or jubilee. On the day of the festivities houses and public buildings are decorated with sycamore and beech branches, evergreens and flowers. Traditional foods include saffron cake, crab salads, Cornish splits with butter and cream and Helston pudding. The pudding has a deliciously light texture and a spicy, fruity taste.

METHOD

Grease a 2 pint/1.1 litre pudding bowl.

Dissolve the bicarbonate of soda in the milk. Mix together all the dry ingredients then add the milk. Stir thoroughly and turn into the prepared bowl.

Cover with a piece of buttered greaseproof paper and place a piece of foil or linen cloth over the top. Tie a piece of string securely around the neck of the bowl to hold the foil or cloth in place. Steam or boil for 2 hours. Serve with custard or the following lemon sauce.

Lemon Sauce

SERVES 5–6

2 rounded tbsp arrowroot
grated rind of ½ lemon
½ pint/1¼ cups/300ml
  water
4oz/½ cup/100g sugar
juice of 2 lemons
3–4 fl oz/about ½ cup/75–
  100ml brandy or sherry

METHOD

Blend the arrowroot with a little of the cold water and add the lemon rind, the rest of the water, the sugar and lemon juice. Bring slowly to the boil, stirring all the time until the sauce thickens. Stir in the brandy or sherry and allow to warm through. Serve hot.

Hindle Wake

FOR THE STUFFING

*8oz/2 cups/225g fresh white
   breadcrumbs*
*1lb/2 cups/450g stoned,
   soaked prunes, roughly
   chopped*

*2oz/½ cup/50g blanched
   almonds, roughly chopped*
*1 tbsp finely chopped fresh
   parsley*
*1 tsp mixed dried herbs
   (marjoram, thyme, basil
   etc.)*
*salt and freshly ground black
   pepper*
2oz/½ cup/50g shredded suet
*¼ pint/½ cup/150ml red
   wine*

1 large boiling fowl
*¼ pint/½ cup/150ml wine
   vinegar*
2 tbsp brown sugar

FOR THE LEMON SAUCE

*1oz/just under ¼ cup/25g
   cornflower (cornstarch)*
1 cup chicken stock (bouillon)
*grated rind of 1 lemon and the
   juice of 2*
*salt and freshly ground black
   pepper*
2 eggs, well beaten
1 extra lemon for decoration

This is a delicious medieval feast day dish which was often cooked at Whitsun. The name is said to have originally been Hen de la Wake or Hen of the Wake. The recipe has changed very little from its medieval origins when chefs were very fond of mixing sweet and savoury foods together with plenty of spices.

Recipes vary a little around the country but all use the dark spicy filling. The chicken was stuffed and boiled slowly overnight, then left to cool. On the evening of the wake's festivities the chicken was lifted out of its broth, coated with a lemon sauce and decorated with prunes and lemon slices.

This turn-of-the-century version of the dish comes from Wigan.

METHOD

Mix all the ingredients for the stuffing together and stuff into the chicken. Sew up the vent securely so that no stuffing can escape.

Place the chicken in a large pan with enough water to almost cover. Add the vinegar and sugar and bring to the boil. Cover and simmer for approximately 3 hours.

Meanwhile, make the sauce. Mix the cornflour (cornstarch) with the stock (bouillon) and bring to the boil. Add the grated lemon rind and juice and the salt and pepper. Boil for 2 minutes then cool slightly.

Stir in the beaten eggs and beat until thick and creamy. When ready to serve reheat but do not allow to boil.

Lift the chicken out of the saucepan on to a serving dish and pour the lemon sauce over. Decorate with lemon slices and a few prunes.

Duck in Cider

SERVES 3–4

FOR THE STUFFING

*4oz/1 cup/100g fresh
    breadcrumbs*
*1 medium onion, chopped and
    softened in oil*
grated rind of 1/2 a lemon
*1/2 tsp dried sage or 4 chopped
    fresh sage leaves*
2 tbsp melted butter
*the duck's liver, finely
    chopped*
*1 stick of celery, finely
    chopped*
*salt and freshly ground black
    pepper*

1 × 4lb (2kg) duck
*salt and freshly ground black
    pepper*
ground ginger
*1/2 pint/1 1/4 cups/300ml dry
    cider*
giblet stock (bouillon)

Roast duck used to be a traditional dish for Whitsun in the West Country. It was eaten with fresh green peas and followed by cherry or gooseberry pie. Other favourites were roast veal or beef. Whitsun was the season for village walks and feasts organized by friendly societies, and everybody would dress in their best and meet together on the village green after the walk to indulge in a huge feast of cold beef and legs of mutton, cold hams, meat pies, pressed beef, pickled onions, salads, jellies, custards and fruit tarts.

METHOD

Preheat the oven to gas 6/200°C/400°F.

First make the stuffing. Mix together all the ingredients and if necessary add a little giblet stock (bouillon) to moisten. Stuff into the duck and secure the opening with thread or skewers.

Prick the duck all over and rub the breast with coarse salt, pepper and a little ground ginger. Place on a rack in a baking or roasting tin. Place in the oven and roast, allowing 25–30 minutes per pound. Every 20 minutes pour off any fat and keep for roasting potatoes etc.

When the duck is ready, remove from the tin and pour off all the fat. Warm the cider and add to the scrapings from the roasting tin with a little giblet stock (bouillon). Season to taste and bring to the boil. Baste the duck with some and serve the rest separately in a sauce boat.

Gloucester Rarebit

SERVES 2

1oz/2 tbsp/25g butter, melted
*4 tbsp grated Gloucester
    cheese*
1 cup pale ale
*4 tbsp fresh breadcrumbs (or
    enough to make the mixture
    as thick as cream)*
*salt and freshly ground black
    pepper*
4 slices of toast

On Whit Monday (or nowadays the Spring Bank Holiday at the end of May) a cheese rolling race is held every year at Coopers Hill near Birdlip in Gloucestershire, when whole Gloucester cheeses are rolled down the hill and chased by competitors. Games like these were once common on Whitsun holidays, but this particular sport is also believed to have its origins in pagan celebrations to welcome the sun back after the winter. Cheeses, like eggs, were seen as symbols of the sun, and so played a part in spring rituals. The Coopers Hill games are also thought to preserve grazing rights on the common land. The large cheeses, weighing anything up to nine or ten pounds, are rolled down the hill, sometimes at sixty or seventy miles an hour. There are four races, and whoever is the first to scramble down and find each cheese, hopefully still intact, can claim it as his or her own.

Preheat the oven to gas 6/200°C/400°F.

Mix together the butter, cheese, ale, breadcrumbs and seasoning and turn into an ovenproof dish. Bake for 25–30 minutes.

Have ready the slices of toast; when the cheese is ready spread liberally on the toast and serve immediately.

White Pot

SERVES 6

4oz/1 cup/100g plain (cake) flour
large pinch of mixed spice
½ tsp grated nutmeg
4oz/2–3 tbsp/100g syrup or black treacle (molasses)
2 eggs, beaten
2 pints/5 cups/1.1 litre milk
½oz/1 tbsp/15g butter
3 fl oz/6 tbsp/75ml cold water or cider

This dish from Gloucester, also called White pont, was made for the Whitsuntide village revels in May, and for the All Souls' Wake at the beginning of November, when villagers sat up all night to pray for the souls of departed friends and relatives. It is very similar to Hasty pudding (see page 35).

METHOD

Preheat the oven to gas 4/180°C/350°F. Grease a deep ovenproof dish.

Mix together the flour, spices, syrup or treacle (molasses), beaten eggs and a little of the cold milk. Bring the rest of the milk to the boil and stir gradually into the flour mixture. Turn into the prepared dish and dot with the butter.

Just before putting the dish into the oven pour the cold water or cider into the middle of the mixture but do not stir.

Bake for 1 hour then lower the heat to gas ¼/110°C/225°F and cook for a further 4 hours. Serve hot.

Oldbury Tarts

MAKES 14–15 TARTS

7fl oz/14 tbsp/225ml boiling
water
3oz/6 tbsp/75g butter or
margarine
3oz/6 tbsp/75g lard
1lb/4 cups/450g plain (cake)
flour
3–4 tsp caster sugar
14oz/2 cups/400g small
gooseberries
2oz/¼ cup/50g demerara
sugar

This recipe comes from Stanway in the Cotswolds, the birthplace of Captain Robert Dover, founder of the once famous Cotswold Games. These started as an athletic event and grew to be an annual meeting that continued from 1612 to 1852. Oldbury tarts were always cooked for the day of the games and for the Whitsuntide festivities, when they followed the traditional roasted ox.

The tarts are made with a hot water crust and are really delicious. The sugary juice from the fruit softens the inside of the pastry while the outside stays crisp.

METHOD

Preheat the oven to gas 6/200°C/400°F. Grease 14–15 patty tins.

Bring the water to the boil and mix with the butter or margarine and lard. Stir until the fats (shortenings) are dissolved. Mix together the caster sugar and flour. Add the liquid and mix with a round-bladed knife to give a pliable dough. Knead for a moment or two then leave to cool a little.

On a lightly floured board roll out the pastry to a thickness of approximately ¼ inch/0.5 cm. Cut 14–15 rounds using a 3 inch/7.5 cm cutter and another 14–15 rounds with a 2½ inch/6 cm cutter. Use the larger circles to line the patty tins.

Fill the pastry cases with gooseberries and sprinkle a little demerara sugar over the fruit. Dampen the edges of the smaller circles with a little water and use to cover the tarts, pressing the damp edges firmly on the base.

Bake for 15–20 minutes until the pastry is a light golden colour. Remove from the oven and serve hot or cold with cream or custard.

(If you don't want to use patty tins this pastry can be moulded with the fingers to make little containers for the fruit and then baked on greased baking trays.)

Goosnargh Cakes

MAKES 16 BISCUITS

*6oz/³⁄4 cup/175g butter,
softened*
*7oz/1³⁄4 cups/200g plain
(cake) flour*
*2oz/just over ¼ cup/50g
caster sugar and more for
dredging*
*2 tsp coriander or caraway
seeds*

These little Whitsun biscuits come from Preston in Lancashire, where it was once estimated that about 50,000 were sold each year. People flocked to the town in horse-drawn carts from nearby towns and villages to eat the cakes and drink the local ale. The biscuits were cooked in huge batches both for Easter and Whitsun, and were flavoured with either coriander or caraway seeds.

METHOD

Preheat the oven to gas 4/180°C/350°F. Grease two baking trays.

Rub or cut the butter into the flour. Add the sugar and coriander or caraway seeds. Work together with the fingertips to make a fairly dry dough.

On a lightly floured board roll out to a thickness of ¼ inch/0.5 cm and cut into rounds using a 2½ inch/6 cm cutter. Dredge the tops with caster sugar and place carefully on the prepared baking trays. Leave room for the biscuits to spread a little.

Bake for 10–15 minutes until pale golden. Remove from the oven and leave to cool on the trays for at least 15 minutes before lifting them carefully on to a wire rack to finish cooling. (They are fairly brittle, so need careful handling.) Dredge the tops again with more caster sugar.

Yorkshire Cheesecakes

MAKES 18 CHEESECAKES

*shortcrust pastry made with
8oz/2 cups/225g plain
(cake) flour. (see page
132)*
2oz/4 tbsp/50g butter
8oz/1 cup/225g curd cheese
*2oz/just over ¼ cup/50g
caster sugar*
1oz/1 tbsp/25g currants
1 tsp grated lemon rind
2 eggs

In May cows produce their maximum yield of milk. In the days before refrigeration, the warm early summer was also the worst time of year to try and keep spare milk. Cheesecakes were an ideal way of using the lactic acid curd produced by soured milk. Throughout Britain little custardy tarts like these were popular at Whitsun and sheep-shearing. At Melton Mowbray in Leicestershire it is said that enough cheesecakes were eaten at the Whitsun festivities to pave the entire town.

METHOD

First make the pastry as on page 132 and chill for at least 15 minutes.

Preheat the oven to gas 4/180°C/350°F. Grease 18 patty tins.

On a floured board, roll out the pastry to a thickness of

approximately ¼ inch/0.5 cm. Using a 2½ inch/7 cm cutter, cut 18 circles and use them to line the patty tins.

Melt the butter and mix with the curd cheese, sugar, currants and lemon rind. Beat the eggs and add to the mixture. Beat well with a wooden spoon.

Spoon the mixture into the pastry cases and bake for 30–35 minutes until the tops are set and just turning golden brown.

Love Feast Cake

MAKES 3 × 2LB/900G CAKES

(It is easier to make this in batches of 3, so freeze one or two of the loaves.)
2lb/900g plain (cake) flour
pinch of salt
6oz/³⁄4 cup/175g butter, softened
6oz/³⁄4 cup/175g lard
1lb/450g sugar
1lb/3 cups/450g currants
4 tbsp candied peel
8oz/1½ cups/225g sultanas
1 tsp mixed spice
2 tsp baking powder
1 tsp bicarbonate of soda
3 eggs
¼ pint/½ cup/150ml milk

In the nineteenth century and the early years of the twentieth, the congregations of Methodist, Baptist and other chapels would go on an annual outing to a local beauty spot to celebrate their solidarity and strength. Anything up to 1500 people would join in prayers and hymns before sharing a feast of cold pies, roast ham, beef, gingerbreads, fruit cakes and this special love feast cake. In the early days it was a fairly plain, yeasted bread, but later it became a richer cake made with baking powder, spice and a lot of dried fruit.

METHOD

Preheat the oven to gas 4/180°C/350°F. Grease 3 × 2lb/900g loaf tins.

Mix together the flour and salt. Rub or cut in the fats (shortenings), then add the sugar, currants, peel, sultanas, spice, baking powder and bicarbonate of soda.

Beat the eggs with the milk and add to the mixture. Mix thoroughly so that all the ingredients are evenly distributed to give a stiff, sticky dough. Knead well then turn into the prepared tins.

Bake for 1–1½ hours until a warm skewer comes out clean. Remove from the oven and leave to cool in the tin for 5 minutes before turning out on to a wire rack to cool completely.

Scripture Cake

Take 4½ cups of 1 Kings IV 22
'and Solomon's provision for one day was
thirty measures of fine flour'
(1lb/450g plain (cake) flour

1½ cups of Judges V 25
'she brought him butter in a lordly dish'
(8oz/1 cup/225g butter)

2 cups of Jeremiah VI 20
'To what purpose cometh there to
me . . . the sweet cane from a far country'
(8oz/1 cup/225g butter)

9 cups of 1 Samuel XXX 12
'and they gave him two clusters of raisins'
(8oz/1½ cups/225g raisins)

2 cups of Nahum III 12
'all thy fortresses shall be like fig trees'
(8oz/1⅓ cups/225g figs)

1 cup of Numbers XVII 8
'the rod of Aaron . . . was budded and put
forth buds, and bloomed blossoms, and bore
ripe almonds'
(2oz/½ cup/50g almonds)

2 tablespoonful of 1 Samuel XIV 25
'and there was honey upon the ground'
(1 tbsp honey)

season to taste with 2 Chronicles IX 9
'And she gave the king . . .spices in great
abundance'
(1–2 tsp mixed spice)

6 cups of Jeremiah XVII 11
'As the partridge gathereth young which she
has not brought forth'
(3 eggs)

a pinch of Leviticus II 13
'with all thine oblations thou shalt offer salt'
(pinch of salt)

½ cup of Judges IV 19
'And she opened a bottle of milk'
(4–5 tbsp milk as required)

2 teaspoonsful of Amos IV 5
'And offer a sacrifice of that which is
leavened'
(1 tsp baking powder)

Follow Solomon's prescription for making a
good boy, Proverbs XXII 14, and you will
have a good cake.
'Thou shalt beat him with a rod'

Many family recipe books of the past contained a recipe for this cake, with quotations from the Bible giving clues to the different ingredients. I found versions of it in old recipe books in Cambridge, Essex, Hampshire and Cornwall. It was usually made for the village church outing on the annual feast day. The day was one of feasting, sport and entertainments as well as of special services often held in the open air, in the church grounds or at a nearby beauty spot. Local bands would play for parades; concerts were given in the chapels; cricket or football matches were played; clay pigeon shoots were held; and there were sometimes fancy dress parades and competitions and side shows and even film shows to entertain the crowds. While all this was going on the village ladies and helpers would prepare the food and lay it out on white linen cloths. There were hams, tongues, cold beef, pies, cakes, buns and biscuits (cookies).

These quantities make a 10 inch/25cm round cake. The amounts in brackets make a better cake than the biblical quantities. The ingredients are not in the order in which they are used, but are as they usually appeared in old recipe books.

METHOD

Preheat the oven to gas 2/150°C/300°F. Grease and line a 10 inch/ 25cm round tin.

Beat together the butter and sugar until light and creamy. Add the eggs and beat thoroughly. Work in the flour, baking powder, spice, salt, raisins, figs (cut into quarters), almonds and honey and add enough milk to give a soft wet mixture.

Turn into the prepared tin and bake for 3 hours until a warm skewer comes out clean. Remove from the oven and leave to cool in the tin for 5 minutes before turning out on to a wire rack to finish cooling.

Clipping Time Pudding

SERVES 4

4oz/²/₃ cup/100g rice
1 pint/2½ cups/600 ml milk
2oz/¹/₃ cup/50g currants
2oz/¹/₃ cup/50g raisins
1½oz/3 tbsp/40g sugar
*a large pinch each of
    cinnamon and nutmeg*
1 egg, beaten
*1 tbsp butter (or marrow
    extracted from 2 cooked
    beef marrow bones) cut into
    small pieces*
pinch of salt

June is the month for sheep-shearing, and on the day that work began, a lavish supper used to be prepared on each farm for the workers and their families. The feast of hams and cold beef, pies, cheeses and home baked bread was held outside whenever possible, and a large separate table was set for the children. The clipping time suppers were apparently a time of great fun and festivity and were often the highlight of the year for the local children. The tradition generally died out during the First World War.

At clipping time suppers in the Lake District, when farmers laid on huge evening meals for the itinerant workers employed for the clipping season, a huge rice pudding was served after the main course. This clipping time pudding was sometimes so big that it would not fit into the farmhouse oven, so it was carried to the village bakery to be cooked there.

One family in Cumbria was so well known for its generous suppers that people would flood in from nearby villages to join the evening's festivities.

METHOD

Grease an ovenproof dish. Preheat the oven to gas 4/180°C/350°F.

Steep the rice in boiling water for 1–2 minutes. Drain and place in the prepared dish with all the other ingredients. Stir well.

Bake for about 2 hours. Serve hot, alone or with cream.

Haymakers' Cocktail

This reviving drink is a Westmorland recipe.

METHOD

Pour the juice slowly into the milk, beating hard. Drink immediately.

*½ pint/1¼ cups/300ml fresh
    orange juice*
*½ pint/1¼ cups/300ml new
    milk*

Apricot Stuffing for Ham

apricots, roughly chopped and the stones removed
an equal quantity of fresh breadcrumbs
salt and freshly ground black pepper
shortcrust pastry made with 1lb/4 cups/450g plain (cake) flour (see page 132)

The apricot crop was always thinned at clipping time. The fruit that was picked was hard and unripe but was ideal for making a stuffing for ham. Fruit stuffed hams were only baked for festive occasions as they did not keep as well as the ordinary smoked and cured hams. A thick pastry crust ensured that the meat did not dry out in a slow oven, and the hardened crust was used after the cooking process to make crumbs to garnish the outside of the ham.

If the apricots are juicy enough they do not need to be cooked before being mixed with the breadcrumbs. Alternatively, dried apricots can be used and should be soaked and lightly stewed before mixing with the bread.

METHOD

Lightly stew the apricots in a little water until the juice begins to run out of the fruit. Mix with the breadcrumbs and seasoning.

Remove the bone from a good piece of ham and press the stuffing into the cavity. Cover the entire ham with a layer of pastry, making sure that it is thick enough to keep all the juices in, and bake for 3½–4 hours at gas 2/150°C/300°F.

Remove from the oven and leave to cool. When completely cold, remove the pastry crust and garnish with pastry crust raspings or baked breadcrumbs.

Haymakers' Beef

SERVES 4

2lb/900g stewing beef, cut
into cubes
1 large onion, peeled and
sliced
a bunch of sweet herbs – basil,
thyme, parsley, a bay leaf,
marjoram
2 cloves
½ tsp ground mace
¼ tsp turmeric
6 whole peppercorns
salt
2.5 fl oz/just over ¼ cup/
65ml wine vinegar
2oz/1½ tbsp/50g black
treacle (molasses)
1 pint/2½ cups/600ml light
ale

This is a traditional early nineteenth-century North Country recipe for haymaking harvest suppers. Large pots of stew were ideal for satisfying the appetites of all the extra itinerant workers who arrived to help with the harvest.

The recipe was very suitable for cooking the rather tough and sinewy meat of an old ox or cow that had come to the end of its working life. Beer and spices help to tenderize the meat and make a deliciously rich and nourishing dish.

METHOD

Place the meat in a large dish or bowl and pile the onion on top. Mix all the other ingredients except the ale and pour over the meat. Marinate for 12 hours or overnight, spooning the liquid over the meat occasionally.

Place everything in a large saucepan and cover with the ale. Bring to the boil and simmer for 3 hours.

Check the seasoning and serve with boiled potatoes, red or white baked cabbage and sweet chutney.

Beltane Bannocks

MAKES 8 BANNOCKS

4oz/just over ¾ cup/100g
oatmeal
a pinch of baking powder
a pinch of salt
1 tsp fat (lard, dripping or
goose fat)
hot water

FOR THE CAUDLE

a little beaten egg
1 tbsp cream
1 tbsp milk
1 tbsp oatmeal

These Scottish oatcakes were cooked in pagan times for the first day of summer on 1 May. Our modern calendar says that summer begins with the summer solstice on 21 June so the bannocks now have a closer link with June than with May. The cakes were originally baked on the Beltane fires that were lit to welcome back the sun after the dark months of winter. They traditionally were made with nine knobs, as described in a manuscript of 1796 which says 'Everyone takes a cake of oatmeal upon which are raised nine square knobs, each dedicated to some particular being, the supposed preserver of their flocks and herds, or to some particular animal, the real destroyer of them. Each person turns his face to the fire, breaks off a knob and, flinging it over his shoulder, says "this I give to thee, preserve thou my horses: this I give to thee, preserve thou my sheep." and so on.'

In the more recent past the bannocks were cooked at the open fire and divided into the number of people present. One piece was blackened with charcoal, lots were drawn and whoever got the black cake was the Beltane Carline (old woman). This poor person would be pelted with eggs for some weeks afterwards and was spoken of as if he or she were dead. This reflects the origins of the baking and eating of the bannock in the days of the druids as far back as 50 AD or earlier. The person who drew the blackened cake was sacrificed to the Celtic gods Taranis the Thunderer and Teutates in a ritualistic killing that involved three blows to the head with an axe, garotting and the burial of the body in water.

The bannocks are made and baked in the same way as oatcakes but they are washed over with a 'Beltane caudle', a thin batter made from egg, milk, cream and oatmeal during the baking process. This makes the bannock wetter and softer than a dry oatcake.

METHOD

Put the oatmeal in a bowl with the baking powder and salt. Make a well in the middle.

Melt the fat and pour into the well. Add enough hot water to make a stiff but pliable dough.

Rub plenty of oatmeal on to the work surface and roll out the dough to a thickness of approximately ⅛ inch/.25 cm. Be careful not to let the surface get sticky, and keep adding more oatmeal if necesssary. Using a 2½ inch/6 cm cutter cut the dough into 8 rounds.

Heat a griddle or heavy frying pan to a steady, moderate heat and cook the bannocks lightly on each side, turning them carefully so that they don't break.

Mix together the caudle, and brush on to one side of the bannocks. Cook this side and while it is cooking brush some of the caudle on to the other side. When the underside is cooked turn and cook the other. Repeat twice so that each side has 3 layers of caudle.

Lift carefully from the pan and leave to cool.

Suffolk Fourses

RECIPE ON PAGE 76

SUMMER

With sheep-shearing and haymaking over for another year, July was a time of relative calm for the farmer. The lull between haymaking and harvest was the time for fairs and parish feast days. Today's fairs have ancient origins going back to the time when public gatherings were associated with temple worship and the offering of sacrifices. On such occasions booths of green branches were built around the sacred area, and there was an atmosphere of celebration. They were often held at the summer solstice, 21 June, the winter solstice, 21 December, and at the end of harvesting, when offerings and sacrifices were made to various pagan gods to ensure a prosperous winter.

With the spread of Christianity throughout Britain these early pagan celebrations were absorbed into the new Christian rituals, and festivities were arranged for the feast day of the patron saint of particular churches. In AD 601 Pope Gregory the Great wrote from Rome to Bishop Mellitus in Britain to urge him to provide solemnities for the English people, so that they could continue their traditional celebrations and build booths of branches and boughs around the temples that had been given over to Christian use. So the rituals persisted under a new guise. They were held annually to commemorate the death of each parish's patron saint, involved two or more days of festivity and were the highlight of the parish year, when everybody expected to have a good time. The Sunday was a day of special church services and the Monday was a public holiday for sports, games and revels.

During the middle ages, the Catholic church had ruled that major saints' days should be fast days, but as these strictures became more and more relaxed so saints' days became an excuse to indulge in all the favourite dishes of beef, ham, veal, roast duckling, pastries, curd tarts, frumenty, plum cakes and gingerbreads that were the staple fare for festive occasions.

The feast days, also later called wakes (after the practice last century of keeping watch in the church on the anniversary of its dedication) and revels, were generally spread over the period stretching from Whit Sunday in May to the end of November, but most were held in late June or early July when the farm was quiet. They continued in many regions until well into this century, as H E Bates wrote in *The Feast of July:* 'We might starve all winter long but the feast was different. Everybody eats till they burst on Feast Sunday.'

Church services and family meals on the Sunday were followed by a holiday for workers and schoolchildren on the Monday, when there were processions with music provided by the local band and itinerant musicians, sporting events, horse races, dances, trading activities and fêtes with colourful side shows. In some places the weekend's celebrations gradually lost their religious significance entirely, and the wakes became merely an excuse for drunken – and sometimes violent – revelry. Elsewhere they retained their religious significance right up to the 1920s and 30s, and in a few counties, notably Cornwall, the annual village feast day still includes an impressive church parade and vast feast dinner on the Sunday, while the various football, rugby and wrestling matches and clay pigeon shoots that used to be held on the Monday have now died out.

The dividing line between religious feast days and commercial fairs was always rather blurred: some of the early gatherings were entirely religious, but most involved not only entertainments but also business. For most traders the great fairs established in medieval times were their main opportunity for distributing their goods, and for most customers they were the only occasion when goods outside the normal supply of everyday foodstuffs were available. They were also great social occasions.

Each fair had its own special treat, such as cheesecake, gingerbread, fair cakes, revel buns, toffee, toffee apples, pies or pasties. Toffee apples are probably the last surviving speciality still to be sold at fairgrounds.

August work on the farms began again in earnest with the beginning of the harvest. Most of the pagan customs associated with the harvest have either disappeared or been swamped by Christian practices. Early Christians celebrated the beginning of harvest on 1 August with a 'festival of the first fruits', when the first corn was ground and made into sacramental loaves which were dedicated to God. The day was known as Llafmaesse, meaning loaf mass, and over the years the name has changed to Lammas. The tradition of a harvest feast dates back to feudal domestic arrangements, when the lord of the manor supplied food and drink to those who had worked especially hard doing 'boon-work'. All the serfs did constant 'week-work', but to provide enough help at times of pressure such as harvest, they were required to work a set number of boon-work days each year. The lord would provide one feast at the end of ploughing and another at the end of harvesting, and the workers were rewarded with food weighed against the value of their work. During the harvest the serfs were fed bread and pottage (a kind of oatmeal gruel), followed by a dish of meat or fish and possibly a lump of cheese, washed down by ale or cider. Basic as this may seem to us today it is far more than most peasants would have been able to afford for themselves during most of the year.

As land ownerships changed over the centuries, individual farmers and their wives took it upon themselves to feed the bands of itinerant workers that arrived each year to help with the harvesting. This season stretched the farm larder enormously, since the workers needed plenty of food to keep them going through a very long working day that started at four or five o'clock in the morning and ended at eight in the evening. The day started with 'first sitting' a pre-breakfast snack, then came breakfast in the fields at eight o'clock. Dinner was at one o'clock and cheesing time or fourses was at four. For these three meals food was carried out to the fields in baskets and linen bags, and the day at the farmhouse must have been a constant round of baking and food preparation. The final meal of the day was supper back at the farmhouse. The food at these suppers, often boisterous affairs, consisted of boiled beef, hams, rabbit stews and pies, roast pork, hotpots of bacon and beans, plum puddings, apple pies, rice puddings, suet figgy puddings, roly-poly puddings, cheesecakes and cheeses, and plenty of ale or cider. The final harvest home supper would be an even more elaborate meal, with toasts to the farmer and his wife, a good deal of drinking, and singing and dancing to the music of fiddles and pipes.

In some areas of Britain the harvest home supper was called a Kern or Kirn feast, the 'kern' being the last handful of corn to be cut. It was popularly believed that the harvest spirit dwelt in the fields, and that as the reapers cut the corn it had to retreat into the remaining crop. The cutting of the last sheaf was therefore surrounded by mystery and a sense of great importance. Once cut the corn was plaited into the form of a woman called a corn dolly, corn or kern baby, maiden, harvest queen, ivy girl, 'neck' or 'mare'. Sometimes it was dressed in a white frock and coloured ribbons and hoisted on to a pole by the strongest or tallest man. In Scotland it was dressed as an old woman, with a white cap, a dress, a little shawl over the shoulders fastened with a sprig of heather and an apron with a pocket stuffed with bread and cheese. This corn dolly took pride of place at the harvest supper and everyone danced with her and drank to her.

Today harvest suppers are still held in parish halls of all denominations around Britain. The idea of a special celebration at church was introduced in 1843 by the Reverend R. S. Hawker, vicar of Morwenstow in Cornwall, who invited his parishioners to receive the sacrament in 'the bread of the new corn', so continuing a tradition that goes back to the days of the early Christians. Today, the harvest supper is more a celebration of the ready supply of food available to us every day, but in those earlier days it had a two-fold significance. It gave the deserving harvesters a chance to let their hair down after all the hard work in the fields and enjoy the plentiful food and drink. It also gave the farmer and his wife a chance to thank the workers for their help in gathering in the vital produce that had to feed the farmer, his family and the livestock through the long cold months of the autumn and winter.

Dorset Jugged Steak

SERVES 5–6

3lb/1.5kg stewing steak

*3–4 tbsp plain (cake) flour
seasoned with salt and
freshly ground black pepper*

1 large onion, sliced

4 cloves

1 tbsp chopped fresh parsley

½ pint/1¼ cups/300ml port

*salt and freshly ground black
pepper*

1 tbsp redcurrant jelly

FOR THE FORCEMEAT BALLS

8oz/1 cup/225g sausagemeat

*3oz/¾ cup/75g fresh
breadcrumbs*

1 egg, beaten

a little plain (cake) flour

1 tsp dried sage

This was an ideal dish for fair day, when everybody was preoccupied with the celebrations, as it could be put into the oven and left to cook very slowly until it was time for the evening meal. This sort of dish is best cooked really slowly so that all the flavours can blend together. It is also ideal for cheaper cuts of meat as the alcohol and slow cooking help to tenderize older, sinewy meat.

METHOD

Preheat the oven to gas 2/150°C/300°F.

Trim the meat of any fat and gristle and cut into cubes. Toss in the seasoned flour and place in a casserole with the onion, cloves, parsley, port, salt and pepper.

Add a little water to almost cover the meat, cover and cook for 2½–3 hours. Check the liquid from time to time to make sure it does not run dry, and if necessary add a little more port or water.

Meanwhile, mix the ingredients for the forcemeat together and, with floured hands, roll into small balls. Heat a small pan of salted water to a steady simmer and drop the forcemeat balls in 7 or 8 at a time. Cook for 10 minutes then lift out with a slotted spoon.

15 minutes before serving the steak, remove from the oven, stir in the redcurrant jelly, add the forcemeat balls and more port or water if needed, and push the balls well down into the gravy.

Increase the oven temperature to gas 4/180°C/350°F. Return the dish, uncovered, to the oven and cook for 15 minutes to brown the forcemeat balls. Serve with mashed turnips or potato.

Squab Pie

FOR THE PASTRY

*12oz/3 cups/350g plain
(cake) flour*
½ tsp baking powder
*6oz/¾ cup/175g butter (or
½ butter and ½ lard)*
1 egg, beaten
salt and pepper

*2lb/900g pieces of boneless
pork*
*1lb/450g onions, peeled and
sliced*
*1lb/450g apples, peeled,
cored and sliced*
1 tsp dried sage
*salt and freshly ground black
pepper*
*1 pint/2½ cups/600ml stock
(bouillon)*

Pies were popular for fair and feast days as they could be made in advance. They were also filling and nourishing, and if they were not eaten one day they would do for the next. In Cornwall there were so many different pies that it was said the devil would never venture into the county for fear of being baked in a pie. There was chipple pie, made with chipples (spring onions or scallions) and bacon; nattlin pie made with pigs' entrails; muggety pie with sheep and calves' entrails; sour-sab pie filled with the stems and leaves of young sorrel; stargazy pie made with young mackerel, herring or sardines; parsley pie; giblet pie; conger pie; herby pie; lamby pie; piggy pie and many more. Squab pie used to be made with young, unfledged pigeons (squabs) and the recipe dates back to medieval days when sweet and savoury were often mixed. Today pork has replaced the pigeon meat: any type of pork meat can be used.

METHOD

First make the pastry. Sift the flour and baking powder together. Cut the fat (shortening) into small pieces and rub or cut into the flour until the mixture resembles fine breadcrumbs. Add the egg, salt and pepper and work to a stiff dough. Knead lightly and chill for at least 15 minutes.

Preheat the oven to gas 7/220°C/425°F. Grease a large pie dish.

Arrange the meat, onions and apples in layers in the dish, adding a little seasoning and sage to each layer. Pour the stock (bouillon) over.

On a floured board roll out the pastry to fit the dish and use to cover the filling. Make a hole in the top and bake for 10 minutes, then reduce the oven temperature to gas 3/170°C/325°F and cook for a further 2 hours. Serve hot or cold.

Forfar Bridies

MAKES 4 PASTIES

FOR THE PASTRY

*12oz/3 cups/350g plain
 (cake) flour*
3oz/6 tbsp/75g margarine
3oz/6 tbsp/75g lard
pinch of salt
water to mix

FOR THE FILLING

*1lb/450g rump steak or
 topside*
3oz/½ cup/75g shredded suet
*2 medium onions, finely
 chopped*
salt and pepper

It is said that these delicious beef pasties were made by Maggie Bridie of Glamis and sold at local fairs and markets. There is also evidence that they were made by a baker by the name of Mr Jolly who had his bakery in the Back Wynd (later Queen Street) in Forfar over a hundred years ago. The pasties are quick and easy to make and they really are extremely tasty.

METHOD

Preheat the oven to gas 5/175°C/375°F. Grease a baking tray.

To make the pastry rub or cut the fats (shortenings) into the flour, add the salt and mix with enough water to give a stiff dough. Divide into 4 equal pieces. On a floured board roll each piece out to a large oval.

Beat the steak flat and cut into ½ inch/1 cm squares. Mix with the suet, onions and salt and pepper and place a quarter of the mixture on each pastry oval, leaving the rim clear for sealing.

Dampen the edges with a little milk or water, fold the pastry over and seal carefully. Make a hole in the top of each, place on the prepared baking tray and bake for 45–50 minutes.

Gooseberry Pudding

SERVES 6

FOR THE SUET CRUST

*10oz/2½ cups/275g plain
 (cake) flour*
pinch of salt
2 rounded tsp baking powder
3oz/¾ cup/75g shredded suet
water to mix

FOR THE FILLING

*1½ pints/3¾ cups/900g
 green gooseberries*
4oz/½ cup/100g sugar

In Bedfordshire and some other counties the first Sunday in July was called Gooseberry Pie or Gooseberry Pudding Sunday, and in Sussex there was always great indignation if the gooseberries weren't ready for puddings and tarts at Whitsun. Bilberries were also made into pies and served with cream. At Lickey in Worcestershire there used to be a Bilberry Wake, and at Egton Bridge in North Yorkshire the Old Gooseberry Show, held on the first Tuesday of August, was a more modern version of the traditional eating of gooseberries at Whitsun.

METHOD

First make the crust. Sift together the flour, salt and baking powder. Add the suet and enough water to give a soft, pliable dough.

Grease a large pudding bowl. On a floured board roll out the dough and use to line the bowl, leaving enough loose dough at the edges to fold over to form a lid.

Top and tail the gooseberries and use to fill the bowl. Sprinkle over the sugar and cover with the pastry edges. Pinch the joints well together.

Cover with greaseproof paper and a linen cloth and tie securely. Steam or boil for 2½–3 hours. Turn out on to a warmed serving dish and serve hot with cream or custard.

Oysters for St James's Day

St James is the patron saint of oysters and those who fish for them, and his feast day has always been celebrated amongst the oyster community with festivities involving the eating of vast quantities of oysters. An old saying maintains that whoever eats oysters on St James's Day will never want for money for the rest of the year.

In Whitstable, for hundreds of years the centre of British oyster production, St James's Day is celebrated with an annual feast on 25 July. At Colchester, the centre of the other major British production area on the Essex coast, the celebrations used to take place on 9 October, the eve of St Deny's day and the start of the second month of the annual oyster harvest. In 1752 the feast day was moved to 20 October. In London St James's Day was celebrated on 5 August, which was known as Oyster Day. In the nineteenth century one hundred million oysters were consumed annually in London alone, many of them on this day. Oysters were such a cheap commodity until the early years of this century that everybody, including the very poor, could afford to eat them regularly. Dr Johnson fed his cat on them for two old pennies a day, and Dickens wrote in *The Pickwick Papers* that 'oysters and poverty always seem to go together'. Tweeny maids in Victorian and Edwardian households begged not to be fed oysters more than three times a week as they grew rather tired of them! How different from today when a dozen oysters cost between £8 and £10 from the fishmonger and even more in restaurants.

Oyster Fritters

SERVES 3–4

12 large oysters

FOR THE BATTER

2 eggs
grated rind of ½ lemon
pinch of nutmeg
pinch of mace
1 tbsp chopped fresh parsley
2 tbsp plain (cake) flour
fat (shortening) or oil for
*   frying*

FOR THE SAUCE

1½oz/3 tbsp/40g butter
1 small onion, finely chopped
1 stick of celery, finely
*   chopped*
2 tbsp plain (cake) flour
oyster liquor
¼ pint/½ cup/150ml milk
1 tbsp dry sherry
2 tsp lemon juice
1 tsp grated lemon rind
salt and freshly ground black
*   pepper*
4 tbsp double (whipping)
*   cream*

Oysters were commonly added to fish and meat stews, forcemeats, stuffings, Lancashire Hot Pot and steak and kidney puddings, as well as being consumed raw in vast quantities, and cooked in dishes on their own. This recipe for oyster fritters dates from 1749 and was called 'ragoo of oysters'. The original sauce is rather heavy and floury so I have adapted it to give a lighter sauce that enhances the flavour of the oysters rather than drowns it. The fritters make an excellent starter.

METHOD

To prepare each oyster hold the shell on a cloth with the hinge towards you and the flatter side uppermost, so that the liquor is contained in the lower, curved shell. Insert the point of a strong oyster knife into the small gap in the hinge and twist the knife to prise the shell open. Slide the knife blade along the inside of the upper shell to cut through the muscles that hold the oyster to the shell. Discard the upper shell and, being very careful not to lose any of the juice or pierce the flesh, clean out any pieces of broken shell with the knife point. Strain the liquor into a bowl and reserve for the sauce. To loosen the oyster hold the shell firmly and run the knife blade under the oyster to sever the lower muscles. Finally, remove the 'beard' – the black gristly part.

Preheat the oven to gas 1/140°C/275°F.

Beat together all the ingredients for the batter. Heat about ¾ inch/1.5 cm of oil or fat (shortening) in a frying pan (skillet). When it is hot, dip each oyster in the batter and fry quickly until golden.

Remove with a slotted spoon and drain thoroughly on kitchen paper. Place on a warm dish and keep hot in the oven while you fry the remaining fritters.

For the sauce, melt the butter in a saucepan and gently fry the onion and celery until soft but not browned. Add the flour and cook, stirring, for 2 minutes.

Gradually add the oyster liquor, milk, sherry, lemon juice, lemon rind, salt and pepper, and simmer for 5 minutes. Stir in the cream and allow to heat through.

Arrange the oyster fritters on individual plates, pour the sauce over and garnish with lemon twists and sprigs of parsley.

Steak and Oyster Pudding

SERVES 5-6

FOR THE SUET CRUST

*7oz/1¾ cups/200g self-
raising (all-purpose) flour*

1 tsp salt

4oz/1 cup/100g shredded suet

freshly ground black pepper

1 tbsp chopped fresh parsley

¼ pint/½ cup/150ml water

FOR THE FILLING

butter for greasing the bowl

*3 tbsp plain (cake) flour
seasoned with salt and
pepper*

*1lb/450g lean beef, cut into
cubes*

*4oz/½ cup/100g lambs'
kidneys with the fat and
gristle removed and thinly
sliced*

1 large onion, finely chopped

*6 large mushrooms, wiped
and sliced*

*8-10 oysters prepared as on
page 58*

2 tbsp chopped fresh parsley

½ tsp grated nutmeg

*1 pint/2½ cups/600ml beef
stock (bouillon)*

Mrs Beeton recommended wrapping the oysters for this pudding inside pieces of steak and then standing the rolls of meat upright in the bowl. It is easier, though, to use the customary chunks of steak and simply to mix the oysters in with the other ingredients.

METHOD

First make the suet crust. Sift together the flour and salt in a large mixing bowl. Add the suet, salt, pepper and parsley and mix with enough of the water to give a light, elastic dough. Knead lightly until smooth.

Grease a 2 pint/1.1 litre pudding bowl with butter. Break off a quarter of the dough and reserve for the lid.

On a floured board, roll out the remaining dough to a circle big enough to line the bowl. Push well down into the basin, making sure that there are no thin patches or breaks in the dough.

Toss the meat in the seasoned flour and fill the bowl with layers of meat, kidney, onion, mushrooms, oysters, parsley and a sprinkling of nutmeg. Pour in the stock (bouillon).

Roll out the remaining dough to form a lid and place on top of the bowl. Seal the edges carefully and cover with a piece of buttered greaseproof paper. Cover with foil or a linen cloth and tie a piece of string around the rim of the bowl to hold the foil or cloth in place.

Steam or boil the pudding for 3½–4 hours. To serve turn out on to a warmed serving dish and have extra gravy ready in a sauceboat.

Gingerbreads

Gingerbread was a standard food at fairs all over Britain, and there are many recipes from the different regions. In Birmingham two gingerbread fairs survived until the beginning of this century. They started in 1251 with a royal charter, granted by Henry III to William Bermingham, which stipulated that the fairs were to be held at Whitsuntide and Michaelmas. Long rows of stalls, clustered around St Martin's church, were loaded with different sorts of gingerbread that were unavailable at other times of the year. Widecombe fair was another very old established fair at which gingerbread and spiced ale were served, and at the main fairs in Norfolk white and brown gingerbread buttons were sold. Norwich fair also sold gingerbread husbands and wives, and gingerbread was popular at the Cambridge Midsummer fair (along with nougat, rock, brandy snaps and winkles).

White Gingerbread

MAKES APPROXIMATELY 20 BISCUITS

2oz/4 tbsp/50g butter
8oz/2 cups/225g plain (cake) flour
3oz/just under ½ cup/75g caster sugar
1 tsp mixed spice
2 tsp ground ginger
pinch of salt
1 egg, beaten
a little milk

This is not really white, but much paler than gingerbreads made with dark treacle.

METHOD

Preheat the oven to gas 4/180°C/350°F. Grease a large baking tray.

Rub or cut the butter into the flour. Add the sugar, spice, ginger and salt. Add the egg and enough milk to give a stiff dough.

On a floured board roll out the dough thinly and cut into small rounds with a pastry cutter. Place on the prepared baking tray and bake for 15 minutes until just browned. Remove from the oven and leave to cool on the tray.

Grasmere Gingerbread

MAKES 16 × 2½ INCH SQUARE PIECES

10oz/2½ cups/275g plain (cake) flour
1 tsp ground ginger
½ tsp ground cinnamon
pinch of salt
4oz/¾ cup/100g chopped dates
5oz/3½ tbsp/150g black treacle (molasses)
3oz/6 tbsp/75g butter
1 egg, beaten
4oz/⅔ cup/100g dark soft brown sugar
¾ tsp bicarbonate of soda dissolved in 3 tbsp milk

Grasmere gingerbread is made for the annual fair held at Grasmere in Cumbria on the Saturday nearest to St Oswald's Day on 5 August. There is a church service on the Saturday, when rushes are strewn on the floor of the church (and left there until the Monday when they are collected by their owners), after which there is a procession from the church to Church Field where, in the past, wrestling matches were held. Nowadays there are sports and tea and the children are all given a piece of gingerbread stamped with an image of St Oswald. The gingerbread is a cross between a sponge cake and a biscuit (cookie), and instead of being rolled out and cut like most early gingerbreads, it is baked in a square tin and cut up after baking.

Crystallized ginger or raisins can be used instead of dates.

METHOD

Preheat the oven to gas 3/170°C/325°F. Grease and line a 10 inch/ 25 cm square tin.

Sift together the flour, ginger, cinnamon and salt. Add the dates.

Melt the treacle (molasses) and butter together over a gentle heat, then leave to cool for a few minutes. Add to the flour and mix thoroughly.

Add the beaten egg, the bicarbonate of soda and the milk, and blend well to a fairly wet, sticky consistency, adding a little more milk if needed. Press into the prepared tin and bake for 1¼–1½ hours until firm and just beginning to darken. Remove from the oven and turn on to a wire rack to cool. While still warm cut into 16 squares.

Mead for St Bartholomew's Day

2 gallons/9 litres water
10lb/4.9kg honey
1½ tbsp brewers' yeast
½oz/4 tsp/15g coriander
*   seeds tied in a muslin bag*
strips of rind from 1 lemon
*   and 1 orange*
7 fl oz/just under 1 cup/
*   200ml brandy*

On 24 August, St Bartholomew's Day, there were fairs and festivities in many regions. The most important was at Smithfield in London, near the present-day Smithfield meat market and St Bartholomew's Hospital. This was originally a medieval cloth fair which received a royal charter in 1215 and continued until 1855. The charter curiously granted alms to the poor of St John's parish nearby, whereas the St Bartholomew's poor who lived on the borders of the fairground enjoyed only the noise, smell and sight of the assembled crowd. There are still fairs on St Bartholomew's day at Carlisle in Cumbria and Newbury in Berkshire.

St Bartholomew is the patron saint of bee keepers and honey makers, and in Cornwall he has played a central role for centuries in the blessing of the mead made by the monks at Gulval near Mount's Bay.

This recipe is from 1815.

METHOD

Heat the water and add the honey. Boil for 1½ hours, removing any scum as it rises.

Leave to cool, and when lukewarm add the yeast, the bag of coriander seeds, lemon and orange rind. Leave to ferment for several days. When the fermenting has stopped, add the brandy and stir well. Strain and pour into clean bottles or a wooden cask and cork tightly. Leave for 6–9 months. For a less sweet mead allow to stand longer.

Eccles Cakes

MAKES APPROXIMATELY 24 CAKES

flaky pastry made with 8oz/2 cups/225g plain (cake) flour (see page 132)

1oz/2 tbsp/25g butter, melted

½ tsp grated nutmeg

2oz/⅓ cup/50g candied peel

8oz/1½ cups/225g currants

4oz/½ cup/100g sugar

These cakes were always associated with the Eccles wakes; the word 'eccles' meant church, and it is believed that they originally had a religious significance and were descended from the special cakes and loaves made as offerings at pagan and early Christian festivals. During the days of the Puritans in the seventeenth century, the eating of such cakes at religious festivals was banned, but surprisingly Eccles cakes survived and continued to be sold at fairs and wakes. The cakes are very similar to several other pastry cakes filled with spiced, dried fruit. Banbury cakes (see page 37) are oval; Hawkshead cakes were as large as a plate; and Chorley cakes are small and round like Eccles cakes. They are all filled with a very similar mixture of currants and sometimes other dried fruits, spices, butter and sugar.

METHOD

Make the pastry as on page 132 and chill for 45 minutes to 1 hour.

Preheat the oven to gas 7/220°C/425°F. Grease 2 baking trays.

Mix together all the ingredients for the filling.

On a floured board roll out the pastry to a thickness of approximately ¼ inch/0.5 cm and cut into rounds approximately 4 inches/10 cm in diameter. Place a spoonful of the filling on each.

Dampen the edges of the pastry, gather together and seal carefully. Turn over and roll gently with a rolling pin to a flat cake. Cut 1 or 2 slits across the top, brush with water and sprinkle with sugar.

Bake for 15–20 minutes until crisp and golden. Remove from the oven and allow to cool on the trays.

Wilfra Week Pie

SERVES 6-8

*shortcrust pastry made with
8oz/2 cups/225g plain
(cake) flour (see page 132)
1½lb/700g apples, peeled,
cored and thinly sliced
4oz/½ cup/100g sugar or
golden syrup
2oz/¾ cup/50g grated
Wensleydale (or other
hard) cheese
a little milk for glazing*

St Wilfred is the patron saint of Ripon, and his feast coincided in the past with the August bank holiday. The festivities included an elaborate procession through the streets of the town to re-enact St Wilfred's entry into Ripon after a long absence abroad. There are two types of cake associated with the festivities. One is this apple and cheese pie and the other is a little almond-flavoured cheesecake called a Wilfra tart, rather like the Hertfordshire pies eaten at Easter (see page 31). It is said that local people would rise early on the morning of St Wilfred's Day – the first or second Saturday of August – and make these little tarts. They were put on dishes outside the front door so that passers-by could help themselves.

This apple and cheese pie is still baked today as an everyday cake and is usually made with the local Wensleydale cheese.

METHOD

Make the pastry as on page 132 and chill for at least 15 minutes.

Preheat the oven to gas 7/220°C/425°F. Grease a swiss roll tin 11 × 7 inches/28 × 18 cm.

On a floured board, roll out half of the pastry to fit the tin and place carefully in the tin. Lightly prick the bottom.

Spread the apples over the pastry and cover with the sugar or syrup. Sprinkle the cheese on top.

Roll out the remaining pastry to fit the tin and use to cover the apples and cheese. Dampen the edges of the pastry and press firmly together. Prick the top and brush with milk.

Bake for 10 minutes, then reduce the oven temperature to gas 4/180°C/350°F and bake for a further 25–30 minutes until golden. Remove from the oven and leave to cool in the tin.

Wakes Cakes and Fairings

Cakes for wakes, revels and festive occasions were often made in large quantities to be given away or sold very cheaply, so they had to be cheap to make. The basis for most of these special occasion cakes was a piece of yeast-leavened dough, taken from the weekly batch of bread dough, which then had added to it whatever extra ingredients were available, such as currants, spices, eggs, butter etc. In the eighteenth century spices and dried fruits gradually became more available and were used instead of large quantities of expensive sugar to sweeten and flavour the cakes. As the years have gone by and as people have become wealthier, festive cakes have become richer and more elaborate and baking powder has replaced yeast. Here are two examples – Ashbourne wakes cakes and Cornish fairings.

Ashbourne Wakes Cakes

MAKES APPROXIMATELY 30 BISCUITS

8oz/1 cup/225g butter, softened
8oz/1 cup/225g sugar
1 egg, beaten
8oz/2 cups/225g self-raising (all-purpose) flour
2 tsp ground ginger
grated rind of 2 lemons
2oz/⅓ cup/50g currants

Preheat the oven to gas 5/190°C/375°F. Grease 2 large baking trays.

Cream together the butter and sugar until light and fluffy. Add the egg and beat well. Add the flour, ginger and lemon rind and mix thoroughly to a soft dough.

On a floured board, carefully roll out the dough thinly and cut into rounds with a 2½ inch/6 cm cutter. Place on the prepared trays, leaving space between the rounds to spread a little during cooking, and press a few currants into each.

Bake for 5 minutes, then reduce the oven temperature to gas 4/180°C/350°F and bake for a further 7–8 minutes until lightly browned. Remove from the oven and leave to cool on the trays for 5 minutes before lifting carefully on to a wire rack to cool completely.

Cornish Fairings

MAKES APPROXIMATELY 24 BISCUITS

8oz/2 cups/225g plain (cake) flour
½ tsp mixed spice
½ tsp ground ginger
2½oz/5 tbsp/65g margarine
1oz/2 tbsp/25g lard
2½oz/6 tbsp/65g demerara sugar
2 tsp bicarbonate of soda
2 tsp cream of tartar
4 fl oz/2½ tbsp/100ml golden syrup, warmed

Preheat the oven to gas 2/180°C/350°F. Grease 2 large baking trays.

Mix together the flour, spice and ginger. Rub or cut in the fats (shortenings) until the mixture resembles fine breadcrumbs. Add the sugar and mix well.

Blend the bicarbonate of soda and the cream of tartar with the warmed syrup and add to the flour mixture. Mix with a fork to a soft paste.

On a floured board roll out to a thickness of ½ inch/1cm and cut out squares or circles with a 2½ inch/6cm cutter. Place well apart on the prepared trays.

Bake for 15–20 minutes until golden and risen. Remove from the oven and leave to cool on the trays for 3–4 minutes before lifting carefully on to a wire rack to cool completely.

Pumpkin Fair Pie

SERVES 6–8

*rich shortcrust pastry made
    with 8oz/2 cups/225g plain
    (cake) flour (see page 132)*
2 eggs
2oz/⅓ cup/50g brown sugar
*½ pint/1¼ cups/300ml
    creamy milk*
½ tsp ground ginger
½ tsp mixed spice
a pinch of ground cloves
1 cup pumpkin purée
*3–4 tbsp double (whipping)
    cream*

The pumpkin fair at Soham in Cambridgeshire dates back to the middle ages. This delicious creamy pumpkin pie was made and sold at the fair.

METHOD

Make the pastry as on page 132 and chill for at least 15 minutes.

Preheat the oven to gas 7/220°C/425°F. Grease an 8 inch/20 cm fluted flan dish.

On a floured board roll out the pastry and use to line the prepared dish.

Beat together the eggs, sugar, milk, spices, pumpkin purée and cream and pour into the pastry case. Bake for 10 minutes then lower the oven temperature to gas 3/170°C/325°F and bake for a further 45 minutes until set. Serve warm or cold with whipped cream.

Sloe Sherry

MAKES 1 × 70CL BOTTLE

sloes
2oz/4 tbsp/50g white sugar
cheap, sweet sherry

Frances Murchison from Lewes in Sussex sent me this recipe for sloe sherry made for sloe fairs in that area. In most parts of the country sloe gin has always been more usual, but this makes a delicious alternative. For the best flavour it needs about six months to mature.

METHOD

Prick the sloes all over with a needle and use to fill a 70cl bottle. Add the sugar and fill up with the sherry.

Cork the bottle tightly and shake daily until the sugar is dissolved. After 6 weeks, strain the sloe sherry through a fine sieve or muslin bag then pour into clean bottles and cork tightly. Keep for at least 3–4 months.

Herring Pie

SERVES 6

*shortcrust pastry made with
1lb/4 cups/450g plain
(cake) flour (see page 132)*
6 fresh herring
a little butter, melted
½ tsp ground mace
*salt and freshly ground black
pepper*
*3 large cooking apples,
peeled, cored and thinly
sliced*
*2 medium onions, peeled and
sliced*

On the Isle of Man herring pie was often served at the harvest home supper, traditionally known as Mheillea. The Manx people have always depended heavily on the success of the herring harvest, and their diet used to consist to a large extent of salt or cured herring. In winter the men of the island worked the land but in summer they all fished for the 'King of the Sea'.

The last sheaf of corn at the Manx harvest was made into a garland, as in the rest of Britain, but instead of being taken to the harvest supper, it was carried by the women reapers to the highest part of the island. Then all the workers, dressed in their best clothes for the harvest supper, enjoyed a huge feast and sang and danced to the music of the fiddler.

This pie can be made with either a potato or a pastry topping. The recipe for this pastry version comes from a late eighteenth-century cookery book.

METHOD

First make the pastry as on page 132.

Preheat the oven to gas 4/180°C/350°F. Grease a large ovenproof dish.

On a floured board roll out two-thirds of the pastry and use to line the prepared dish. Roll out the remaining third of the pastry to make a lid.

Scale, gut and clean the herring and remove the heads, fins and tails. Put a little butter in the bottom of the pastry case and lay the herring on top. Season with mace, salt and pepper. Add the apples, then a layer of onions and add a little more butter.

Pour in a cup of water and cover with the pastry lid.

Bake for 35–40 minutes.

Fidget Pie

SERVES 4

*shortcrust pastry made with
8oz/2 cups/225g plain
(cake) flour etc. (see page
132)*

*1lb/450g potatoes, peeled and
thickly sliced*

*8oz/just over 1 cup/225g
bacon, diced or cut into
small, thin slices*

*1lb/450g apples, peeled,
sliced and dipped in sugar if
very sour*

*salt and freshly ground black
pepper*

½ tsp grated nutmeg

*½ pint/1¼ cups/300ml
water*

This fidget or fitchett pie is a Shropshire speciality, but similar pies were also served in Lincolnshire, Cambridgeshire and elsewhere as a supper dish for harvesters. The pie was suitable for cheaper cuts of mutton or ham so the workers could be fed cheaply but very well. A Cambridgeshire recipe uses cider instead of stock (bouillon) and this Shropshire recipe seems to be the only one to include potatoes.

METHOD

First make the pastry as on page 132.

Preheat the oven to gas 7/220°C/425°F. Grease a large pie dish.

Place a layer of potatoes in the bottom of the dish, then place on top a layer of bacon, then a layer of apples, adding a little nutmeg and seasoning between the layers.

Repeat the layers until the dish is full. Pour the stock (bouillon) over.

On a floured board roll out the pastry quite thickly and use to make a lid for the pie. Make a hole in the middle and bake for 20 minutes. Reduce the heat to Gas 4/180°C/350°F and bake for a further 30–40 minutes until crisp and golden.

Soused Mackerel

SERVES 4

3–4 mackerel

¼ pint/½ cup/150ml water

2 bay leaves

salt

*½ pint/1¼ cups/300ml wine
vinegar*

12 peppercorns

a few whole allspice

One of the main mackerel fishing areas in Dorset is off Chesil Bay at Abbotsbury, where this dish of soused mackerel is popular at harvest time. At Southend the whitebait harvest is celebrated in September with a 'Blessing the Catch' ceremony held on a trawler moored off the pier. At Musselburgh, Midlothian, the second Friday in September is the harvest festival of fishermen, when the village is decorated with garlands and flags, the fishing fleet lies at its moorings and local bands play music for dancing in the streets. The women and girls traditionally wear striped petticoats, turned-back dresses and shawls, and carry small dolls which are dressed as fisherwives.

METHOD

Preheat the oven to gas 2/150°C/300°F.

Clean and wash the fish, remove the backbone and head and roll up, finishing with the tail end. Secure each roll with a cocktail stick.

Pack the rolls tightly into an earthenware dish. Add all the other ingredients, cover and bake for 1 hour.

Cool and store the fish in the liquor, in the refrigerator, until needed.

Eat as a starter or a lunch dish with thin slices of brown buttered bread and/or salad.

Jugged Hare

SERVES 4

1 young hare, cleaned (reserving blood from the chest), wiped and cut into neat pieces

2–3 tbsp plain (cake) flour seasoned with salt and freshly ground black pepper

2oz/4 tbsp/50g butter

8 fl oz/1 cup/225ml port

1 large onion, peeled and sliced

1 strip of lemon peel

3 allspice

½ tsp freshly ground black pepper

2 tbsp plain (cake) flour

2 tsp mushroom ketchup (catsup) (optional)

forcemeat balls (see page 54)

Hare was another favourite meat for harvest suppers and it was cooked in similar dishes to rabbit. There is more meat on a hare and it therefore fed more people. It was quite common in the past to roast a hare whole. The animal was usually stuffed with herbs, bacon, lemon peel, anchovies, the liver, suet, breadcrumbs and spices or herbs. As it cooked it was basted with cider, beer or milk, and it was served with a good gravy. For harvest, however, it was more usual to joint it and jug it in port with plenty of spices, or to stew it gently in beer and serve it with gravy and redcurrant jelly. In some areas hare was also popular as a Christmas dish.

This old Cambridgeshire recipe can also be made with rabbit.

METHOD

Dredge the hare joints with seasoned flour and fry in the melted butter. Place in a large pan with the port, onion, lemon peel, allspice, pepper and enough water barely to cover.

Mix the blood from the hare's chest with the flour and a little cold water. Mix thoroughly and pour into the pan.

Bring slowly to the boil, stirring all the time, then cover and simmer very gently for 3–4 hours, until tender.

Make the forcemeat balls as on page 54 and fry in a little oil or dripping. Add to the stew 5–10 minutes before serving.

When the hare is ready, lift the meat from the pan on to a serving dish and keep warm. Thicken the gravy if necessary and add the mushroom ketchup (catsup), if using. Bring to the boil, adjust the seasoning and strain over the meat. Serve with redcurrant jelly.

Harvest Rabbit

SERVES 4

2 small rabbits, cut into pieces
   approximately 3 inches long

oil or dripping for frying

1/2 a prune for each piece of
   rabbit

a thin strip of fat bacon for
   each piece of rabbit

2–3 tbsp plain (cake) flour
   seasoned with salt and
   pepper

2 large onions, peeled and
   thinly sliced

2 bouquets garnis

stock (bouillon)

forcemeat balls (see below)

FOR THE FORCEMEAT BALLS

2 rashers of bacon, roughly
   chopped

5oz/1 1/4 cups/150g fresh
   breadcrumbs

2 tbsp chopped fresh mixed
   herbs (chives, parsley,
   marjoram etc.)

salt and freshly ground black
   pepper

1 egg, beaten

Doris Ling, writing to me from Suffolk about her childhood, said that 'Harvest time of course brought a great deal of rabbit dishes in many forms. We also had home-made pork cheeses (or brawn) and pigs' trotters cooked.' Farmers' wives took advantage of all the rabbits shot in the fields during harvesting, so rabbit pies, jugged rabbit, rabbit stews and rabbit brawn were all popular.

This recipe for harvest rabbit stew was sent to me by Sylvia Legge of Windermere, Cumbria.

METHOD

Wash the rabbit pieces and soak in salted water for about 15 minutes. Dry well.

Preheat the oven to gas 3/170°C/325°F.

Melt a little dripping or oil in a pan and fry the rabbit pieces until golden brown. Drain well.

Wrap each piece of rabbit with half a prune inside a strip of bacon. Coat thickly with seasoned flour.

Place the sliced onion in the bottom of an ovenproof dish and place the rabbit pieces on top with the bouquets garnis. Add enough stock (bouillon) just to cover. Bake for 2–2½ hours.

Meanwhile, make the forcemeat balls. Mix all the ingredients together thoroughly and shape with floured hands into fairly large balls.

Heat a little oil and fry until brown all over. Keep hot until ready to serve. When the rabbit is ready. Serve on a large dish surrounded by the forcemeat balls. Serve with mashed potatoes and vegetables.

Harvest Pot

SERVES 6–8

*8oz/1½ cups/225g dried
  beans – white haricots,
  butter beans or broad beans*
*1½lb/700g lamb, cut into
  chunks*
*1½lb/700g lean pork, cut
  into chunks*
dripping or oil for frying
*2 slices smoked bacon, cut into
  small pieces*
*2 large onions, peeled and
  thinly sliced*
*salt and freshly ground black
  pepper*
2 tsp dried mixed herbs
4 medium tomatoes
*8oz/2 cups/225g fresh
  breadcrumbs*

This was a typical harvest dish, made with whatever cuts of meat were available, and padded out with beans to feed all the extra harvest workers. Beans have been a standard ingredient of British cooking since the middle ages, particularly in winter when salted meat was used. Salt meats were soaked in several changes of water to remove some of the excess salt before being cooked, but rice or pulses were needed to absorb what was left in the meat.

This dish was popular in the Cambridge area.

METHOD

Pour boiling water on to the beans and leave to soak overnight. Drain, place in a pan of fresh water, bring to the boil and simmer for 10 minutes.

Preheat the oven to gas 5/190°C/375°F.

Heat the dripping or oil in a frying pan (skillet) and brown the lamb and pork on all sides. Strain the beans and reserve the liquor.

Put layers of beans, meat, bacon and onions into a large ovenproof dish, adding some of the herbs and seasoning to each layer.

Skin and slice the tomatoes and lay on top of the meat. Pour over the bean liquor and scatter the breadcrumbs over the top. Cook for 1½ hours until the meats are tender.

Potato Harvest Pudding
(Poten Ben Fedi)

SERVES 4–5

2lb/900g potatoes, boiled and mashed

1oz/2 tbsp/25g butter

1 tbsp plain (cake) flour

a little oil for frying

1 large bacon rasher, cut into small pieces

1 large onion, peeled and chopped

6oz/³/4 cup/175g minced (ground) cooked meat

salt and freshly ground black pepper

In Wales this was a traditional Sunday supper dish for the end of the potato harvest in late September and October.

In Lancashire the farmers' wives fed the potato pickers with potato cakes made from grated potatoes mixed with a little flour, salt and milk and fried in hot fat (shortening) until golden. These were carried out to the fields in baskets. Evening meals during the harvest and at the final harvest home supper usually included Lancashire hotpot made with local potatoes. In many other regions of Britain the end of the potato harvest was celebrated with a supper of new boiled potatoes in the farm kitchen. Plenty of fresh butter and milk were put on the table and everybody helped themselves. Another popular dish was potato pie made by baking sliced onions and potatoes under a shortcrust pastry lid. In Ireland, harvest festival was held on the last Sunday in August and the harvest supper was a feast of new potatoes, bacon and cabbage.

METHOD

Preheat the oven to gas 5/190°C/375°F. Grease a pie dish.

Mix the mashed potato with the butter and flour.

Heat the oil and fry the bacon and onion. When the onion is soft but not browned add it to the potato with the minced (ground) meat, salt and pepper. Mix well so that all the ingredients are evenly distributed.

Turn the mixture into the prepared dish and bake for 30 minutes until golden and crispy. Serve hot.

Hasty Harvest Pudding

SERVES 5–6

FOR THE BASE

1oz/2 tbsp/25g butter

1lb/450g cooking apples, peeled, cored and sliced, or rhubarb, washed and cut into small pieces

1oz/2 tbsp/25g sugar

grated rind of 1 small lemon

This was a traditional dish for the beginning of the harvest, when the first sheaves of corn were carried in. The pudding is a rather more elaborate variation of the hasty pudding made for Whitsun. Whereas the Whitsun pudding was a basic mixture of butter, flour, sugar and milk, this has a base of fresh apples or rhubarb and a spicy topping. This recipe was sent to me by Jenny Marsland of Sark in the Channel Islands.

FOR THE MIDDLE

1oz/2 tbsp/25g butter
1oz/4 tbsp/25g plain (cake)
  flour
1oz/2 tbsp/25g sugar
1 egg, beaten
3/4 pint/13/4 cups/450ml milk

FOR THE TOPPING

2oz/just over 1/4 cup/50g
  demerara sugar
1/2 tsp ground cinnamon
1/2oz/1 tbsp/15g butter

METHOD

Grease a 1½ pint/3¾ cups/900ml ovenproof dish.

For the base, melt the butter in a pan and add the apples or rhubarb and sugar. Cook over a low heat until soft and pulpy. Remove from the heat and add the lemon rind. Pour into the prepared dish.

For the middle, melt the butter in a pan and add the flour. Cook over a low heat for 2 minutes, stirring all the time, then gradually add the milk.

Bring to the boil, stirring all the time then simmer for about 2 minutes. Remove from the heat and beat in the sugar, and then the egg, a little at a time.

Return to the heat and cook for 1 minute, stirring all the time. Pour over the apples or rhubarb.

For the topping, mix together the sugar and cinnamon and sprinkle over the pudding. Cut the butter into small pieces and dot over the top. Place under a moderate grill until the sugar topping turns brown. Serve hot or cold.

Boiled Plum Pudding

SERVES 8–10

2 eggs
1/2 pint/11/4 cups/300ml milk
1lb/4 cups/450g plain (cake)
  flour
1lb/4 cups/450g shredded suet
6oz/3/4 cup/175g sugar
4oz/2/3 cup/100g currants
8oz/11/2 cups raisins
1 tsp mixed spice
a pinch of salt
1 tbsp black treacle (molasses)

This is rather like a Christmas pudding but not quite so rich, and was a favourite at harvest suppers. Early recipes for boiled plum puddings did actually contain plums or prunes, but these were later replaced by dried fruit such as raisins, currants and sultanas as these became more readily available. The pudding was ideal for harvest suppers as it helped to satisfy the appetite of all the hungry harvesters when they came in from their day's work in the fields. Other popular puddings included jam roly-poly, suet figgy pudding and thick rice puddings.

This is an Oxfordshire recipe from the mid-nineteenth century.

METHOD

Grease a large pudding bowl.

In the bowl beat the eggs and add the milk. Add all the other ingredients and stir thoroughly. Cover the bowl with greaseproof paper and a linen cloth tied firmly around the neck of the bowl with a piece of string.

Steam or boil for 5–6 hours. To serve, turn out on to a warmed serving dish and serve with custard and cream.

Hop-pickers Cake

MAKES 2 × 1LB/450G OR 1 × 2LB/900G CAKE

10oz/2½ cups/275g self-raising (all-purpose) flour

1 tsp mixed spice

1 tsp ground ginger

6oz/¾ cup/175g margarine

4oz/⅔ cup/100g soft brown sugar

4oz/⅔ cup/100g currants

4oz/⅔ cup/100g sultanas

2oz/⅓ cup/50g mixed candied peel

¾ pint/2¾ cups/450ml milk

½ tsp bicarbonate of soda

1 tsp cream of tartar

1 tbsp black treacle (molasses)

This recipe was very kindly sent to me by Jack Hamilton, editor of *Folk in Kent*. It was contributed to the magazine by Jane Hamilton and was printed in the January 1988 edition. The cake was made to feed the hop-pickers during the harvest and, like seed cakes and plum breads, was carried out to the hop fields in baskets at lunch and tea time.

A note from Jane Hamilton says that the cake is inclined to sink in the middle but keeps very well. When I made it I was sure that all the fruit would sink to the very bottom because the mixture is very runny when it goes into the tin, but I was wrong. The fruit stayed where it should and the cake did not sink. It is a deliciously moist, spicy cake with plenty of fruit.

METHOD

Preheat the oven to gas 3/170°C/325°F. Grease 2 × 1lb/450g or 1 × 2lb/900g loaf tin and line with greaseproof paper.

Sift together the flour and spices. Rub or cut in the margarine and add the sugar and fruit. Mix well.

Warm the milk with the bicarbonate of soda, cream of tartar and treacle. Pour into the flour and fruit and mix thoroughly. The mixture should drop from the spoon.

Pour into the prepared tins and bake for approximately 1½ hours for the 1lb/450g cakes and 1¾ hours for the 2lb/900g cake until a warm skewer comes out clean. Remove from the oven and leave to cool in the tins.

Rich Seed Cake

**MAKES 1 × 8 INCH/20 CM
ROUND CAKE**

*8oz/1 cup/225g butter,
  softened*
6oz/⅞ cup/175g caster sugar
*8oz/2 cups/225g plain (cake)
  flour*
*1½oz/3 tbsp/40g caraway
  seeds*
3 eggs

All sorts of seed cakes were made around Britain at harvest time and carried out to the workers in the fields in baskets and linen cloths. Other cakes made to keep the workers going were heavy cake made with lard, peel and currants, plum cake with plenty of dried fruit, jam buns, apple turnovers, yeasted buns, saffron buns and nodden cake, a sort of pastry, eaten spread with butter. Fruit tarts, filled with local plums or apples and blackberries, were also popular.

This recipe is from Frome in Somerset and dates back to 1852.

METHOD

Preheat the oven to gas 4/180°C/350°F. Grease and line an 8 inch/20 cm round cake tin.

Cream the butter and sugar until light and fluffy. Add the flour and seeds and beat well.

Whisk the eggs and fold into the cake. Beat for 3–4 minutes to incorporate plenty of air into the mixture. Turn into the prepared tin and bake for 1¼ hours until a warm skewer comes out clean.

Remove from the oven and leave to cool in the tin for about 15 minutes before turning out on to a wire rack to cool completely.

Harvest Cocktail

*4oz/just over ¾ cup/100g
  oatmeal*
6oz/¾ cup/175g sugar
juice of 1 lemon
*1 gallon/20 cups/4.8 litres
  boiling water*
½ oz/4tsp/15g ground ginger

Farmers often provided cider for the harvesters, and sometimes beers brewed from combinations of local herbs – yarrow, sage, dandelion leaves, young nettles – with yeast and sugar added.

This was a forerunner of commercially produced barley water.

METHOD

Put the oatmeal and sugar into a saucepan and add the lemon juice and a little warm water. Mix well, then add the boiling water and ginger. Boil together for 3 minutes, stirring all the time.
Strain and cool. Serve chilled with ice and slices of lemon.

Suffolk Fourses

**MAKES APPROXIMATELY
10 CAKES**

1oz/4 tsp/25g fresh yeast
1 tsp caster sugar
½ pint/1¼ cups/300ml milk
2oz/4 tbsp/50g lard
*2lb/8cups/900g plain (cake)
   flour*
½ tsp salt
4oz/½ cup/100g sugar
*4oz/½ cup/50g currants or
   raisins*
a pinch of mixed spice
6oz/¾ cup/175g butter
3 eggs, well beaten
*caster or demerara sugar for
   dredging*

In Suffolk this cake was eaten with tea or home-made lemonade when the harvesters took a break from work in the middle of the afternoon. There are many variations from around the county: one from Bury St Edmunds is a very plain cake, but most are doughy, curranty cakes cut into rounds, each round being divided into four sections by knife markings made before baking. The rounds were sprinkled with sugar and carried out to the workers in baskets or bags. I dredge the cakes before baking so that the sugar stays on the top. They are very good eaten on their own but they are also delicious split and spread with butter and jam or honey.

METHOD

Cream the yeast with the caster sugar. Warm the milk and add to the yeast.

Rub or cut the lard into the flour and salt, then add the sugar, raisins or currants and mixed spice.

Melt the butter and mix with the beaten eggs. Add to the warm milk and yeast mixture. Pour into the flour and mix with a round-bladed knife to make a light dough.

Cover with a damp cloth and set in a warm place for about 2 hours to rise. Grease two baking trays.

When the dough has doubled in size, knead on a floured board. Roll out to a thickness of approximately ¾ inch/2 cm and cut into 4 inch/10 cm rounds.

Place on the prepared baking trays and leave in a warm place for 30 minutes to prove. Meanwhile preheat the oven to gas 6/200°C/400°F. When the dough has risen, dredge the tops with caster or demerara sugar mark into 4 sections and bake for 15–20 minutes until firm and golden.

Remove from the oven and leave to cool on the trays.

Cream Crowdie

SERVES 4

*1 pint/2½ cups/600ml double
(whipping) cream
medium oatmeal, lightly
toasted in a dry saucepan
over a moderate heat
demerara or soft brown sugar
Scotch whisky*

Cream crowdie is a very old Scottish recipe served in farmhouses on festive occasions, especially at harvest home suppers when the crops had all been gathered in. The name 'crowdie' probably derives from the Gaelic 'cruaidh', meaning thick and firm, and it was used for all porridge-like foods made with oats. Crowdie was once the staple breakfast food in Scotland, and 'crowdie time' came to mean time to eat or breakfast time. In the Highlands crowdie is a kind of soft cheese made from skimmed milk.

Sometimes a ring was hidden in the cream crowdie and traditionally whoever found it would be the first to wed. After the harvest supper there was dancing, singing and drinking, and at midnight dishes of herring and potatoes were served.

METHOD

Beat the cream until light and frothy, and give a bowlful to each person. The idea is that everyone helps themselves to as much of the oatmeal, sugar and whisky as they like, mixing it into the cream.

AUTUMN

When harvesting was over at the end of September, farmers took stock and calculated how much fodder was available to feed the livestock through the winter, and therefore how many animals to keep and how many to sell or slaughter. Autumn was consequently a time for markets and fairs where surplus animals were sold. It was also the time of year when farm labourers found themselves out of work and either had to renew their contract with their current employer or find a new position. To do this they would go to the hiring fairs that were held throughout Britain on or near Michaelmas on 29 September. St Michael's Day was a quarter day, when bills and rents were paid and contracts completed or renewed. The hiring fairs acted as a sort of primitive labour exchange, where each labourer wore something that indicated his or her calling. A wagoner would wear a piece of whipcord, a cowman a whisp of hay, a shepherd a tuft of wool and a housemaid a strand or two from a mop. Dressed in their best, they would stand and wait for prospective employers to approach them.

Michaelmas was a very important time of year for everybody, and a day of feasting and celebration. Roast goose was the traditional dish, served with all sorts of stuffings and sauces. Goose was also the favourite meal for Martinmas on 11 November, a feast day that marked a great ecclesiastical festival originated by Pope Martin I in the seventh century, and which linked with ancient new year celebrations.

The three days from 31 October to 2 November are celebrated with a mixture of pagan and Christian festivities. The pre-Christian festival of Samhain celebrated the end of summer and the beginning of the Celtic new year on 1 November. Surplus livestock was killed off for winter food and the sheep were mated to provide the following year's new lambs. It was believed to be a time when natural laws were suspended and evil spirits, ghosts, witches and demons roamed free: new Beltane fires were kindled to drive away evil influences and to give symbolic strength to the dying sun, and to ensure that the earth would awake again at the end of its long winter sleep. It was also a time of divination and fortune-telling: young girls tried by all sorts of ritualistic games and activities to find out who their future husbands would be; and farmers attempted to predict the weather in the coming months.

Many of these pagan activities were absorbed into the Christian church, and the earlier rituals have continued alongside Christian celebrations. The first of November is All Saints' Day and 31 October became Hallowe'en or All Hallows' Eve, a day of feasting and festivity before the fast day when all the saints, especially those who have no particular feast day, are honoured. 'Hallow' means holy, and All Saints' Day was once known as All Hallow Mass. All Souls' Day is on 2 November, when prayers are offered for the dead. So All Saints' Day is also All Souls' Eve. In pagan days the last day of the old year, 31 October, was the time when the dead returned home to eat and drink. This was a widespread belief throughout Europe. The Beltane fires were thought to bring comfort to souls in purgatory, and prayers were said while bundles of burning straw were held up high.

In England the day of bonfires on 5 November was appropriated for celebrating the foiling of the gunpowder plot in 1605. Now known as Bonfire Night or Guy Fawkes Night, it has really taken over from Hallowe'en. In Ireland Hallowe'en has remained the important celebration, as the Irish do not mark the foiling of a Roman Catholic plot and therefore have no Guy Fawkes Night. In Wales, Scotland and the Isle of Man, too, the Celtic festival has retained its significance and importance. The festivities and rituals of the three days of Hallowe'en, All Saints' Day and All Souls' Day may have become rather confused over the centuries, but the elements of warding off evil spirits, making offerings to the dead, divining fortunes and foreseeing future marriages have continued to the present day in many parts of Britain.

In Ireland, Hallowe'en is celebrated with all sorts of special dishes – apple dumplings, potato apple cake, boxty pancakes made with potatoes and flour, dumplings made with potatoes, potato pudding, colcannon made with mashed potatoes and cabbage, barm brack (a fruity loaf), apples and nuts. Whatever the dish eaten on Hallowe'en night, a wedding ring is carefully wrapped in greaseproof paper and hidden in it. Whoever finds the ring will be the first to marry. The same ritual is observed in most parts of Wales and Scotland. To see her future husband's face a young girl must look into the mirror while combing her hair and eating an apple. To find out his name she must peel an apple and throw the unbroken strip of peel over her shoulder. The initial of the name can be read in the twisted peel. In Scotland, the Isle of Man and some parts of England a 'dumb cake' is baked to enable young women to divine their future husband. In Scotland the cake was made of oats, flour and water, and was baked in the ashes and eaten in silence while walking backwards to bed. Any number of girls could join in, and all would dream of the man they would marry. In the Isle of Man the cake (*soddag valloo*) was a mixture of flour, eggs, egg shells, soot and salt, kneaded to a dough and eaten in silence as in Scotland. A salted herring stolen from a neighbour and cooked in its brine could be used in the same way.

In Scotland, other Hallowe'en dishes included champit tatties (mashed potatoes), cooked apples, mashed turnips (neeps), gingerbread, special Hallowmas bannocks made with oatmeal, and buttered sowans. These were made by soaking the inner husks of oat grains in lukewarm water for three or four days until sour. The liquor was then drained off and the seeds thrown away. The liquor was left to stand to allow the starchy matter to sink to the bottom. This solid part was called sowans and the liquid was swats. The swats were drained off and the sowans were put into a pan with as much water as was needed to thin them. A little salt was added and they were boiled for ten minutes until they thickened. For Hallowe'en they were cooked with butter and served with the traditional wedding ring concealed in them.

In the Isle of Man, Hallowe'en was always celebrated on 11 November, the correct date in the Old Celtic calendar. It is known as Hollantide or Hop-tu-Naa (believed to derive from the same linguistic origins as Hogmanay). Several of the Manx new Celtic year rituals were very similar to Scottish Hogmanay celebrations. Mummers would go from house to house knocking on doors with turnips and cabbages on sticks, singing special songs and hoping to be given potatoes, herrings and bonnags (oat cakes). Nowadays Hallowe'en is celebrated as elsewhere on 31 October, and the children carry turnip lanterns from house to house. The traditional supper is a variation of the colcannon that is eaten in Ireland and Scotland, and consists of potatoes, parsnips and fish mashed together. Any unfinished food is left on the table for the fairies. In the English West Country Hallowe'en is called Punkie Night, after the pumpkins that are hollowed out to make lanterns. These were originally intended to represent the souls of the dead.

Special foods throughout Britain for All Souls' Day on 2 November consist mainly of special bread called Saumas loaves (from Soul Mass) and soul cakes, which were usually small round flat spiced buns. In Yorkshire they were small fruit cakes and in Northamptonshire they were made with caraway seeds. The bread and cakes are both thought to be relics of the food that was left in graves for the dead in pagan times. In some areas, housewives baked large batches of soul bread and cakes and offered them to anyone who called at the house during All Souls' Day. In other regions, mummers or guisers, with blackened faces and dressed in the clothes of the opposite sex, would go round in groups begging for money and cakes.

Three other major festivals fall very close to each other in November: 23 November is St Clement's Day, traditionally called Clemeny or Clementy. In Staffordshire it was customary to drink 'lambs wool', a festive wassail bowl of spicy hot beer with floating apples (see page 129). In Wantage, Essex, little clementy cakes were baked every year until about 1895. In Wales the traditional feast dish of roast goose was followed by a rich rice pudding.

Two days later came St Catherine's Day. Also called St Kattern, Katern or Catern, St Catherine is the patron saint of spinners, and was adopted by lace-makers in Nottinghamshire, Bedfordshire and Buckinghamshire. This was their major festival and holiday until well towards the end of the last century: women would dress in men's clothing, sing traditional working songs and visit neighbours. There they were fed cattern cakes (also known as wiggs) and a drink of warmed beer beaten with eggs and rum. Later in the evening there would be a feast of pork chops decorated with apple rings, and then there were games and a firework display with plenty of Catherine wheels. In Peterborough the children were fed steak and onions for their midday meal and there was a party after tea.

The Cattern Day celebrations spilled over into the festivities for St Andrew's Day five days later. St Andrew is the true patron saint of lace-makers, and in most districts other than those for whom St Catherine's Day was the major feast, 30 November was a day for important celebrations. People would congregate in each other's houses, where they ate frumenty (see page 128) and drank methaglin, a mead-like drink with spices and ground malt. Tanders cakes were made from a similar mixture as cattern cake – a bread dough with added fat (shortening), caraway seeds and sugar. Other special dishes in the lace areas included figs, hot elderberry wine and sweets called black buttons.

St Andrew's Day, 30 November, is of course a day for celebration in Scotland. Before the sixteenth century it was a religious holiday, but since the Reformation it has been given over simply to eating, drinking and merry-making. The festivities of the past included special meals of haggis, singed sheep's head, minced collops and rabbit or fish pies. Once all these saint's day celebrations were over there were only the four weeks of Advent until the most important celebrations of the year. Now came the time to make the rich Christmas pies, puddings and cakes to give them plenty of time to mature before 25 December.

Michaelmas Goose

SERVES 6–8

1 × 8–9lb/4–4.5kg goose,
cleaned and trussed ready
for the oven
1 lemon, cut into 4
1 tsp salt
½ tsp freshly ground black
pepper

FOR THE STUFFING

6 large potatoes, cooked and
mashed
1 medium onion, finely
chopped
4 rashers streaky (side)
bacon, finely diced
1 tsp salt
½ tsp freshly ground black
pepper
12oz/1½ cups/350g pork
sausagemeat
1 tbsp chopped fresh parsley
1 tsp chopped fresh thyme or
½ tsp dried thyme
1 tsp chopped fresh sage or ½
tsp dried sage

giblets boiled to make stock
(bouillon)
¼ pint/½ cup/150 ml dry
cider

After the harvest, the geese went 'a-stubbling'; that is, they were sent into the fields of stubble to eat the grain that was left lying around. By the time of Michaelmas, on 29 September, the geese were in prime condition. Tenants paid their landlords with fattened stubble geese and kept the inferior pasture-fed geese for themselves.

The origins for the custom of eating goose at Michaelmas are said by some to stem from the fact that Queen Elizabeth I happened to be eating goose on St Michael's Day when Francis Drake brought her the news of the English victory over the Spanish Armada. The real explanation is likely to be simpler: the goose was ready for eating at this time of the year and St Michael's feast day was the ideal excuse. It has become the standard dish for the festivities.

This recipe is the traditional Irish method of cooking the goose, and uses a potato stuffing which helps to soak up some of the grease from the bird. A little cider added to the gravy gives it a delicious flavour and also helps cut the greasiness.

METHOD

Preheat the oven to gas 8/230°C/450°F.

Prick the goose all over with a fork. Rub the skin with ¾ of the lemon. Squeeze the juice from the last ¼ into the cavity of the goose. Rub the skin with salt and pepper.

Mix together the ingredients for the stuffing so that all are evenly distributed. Pack the stuffing into the goose and sew up the opening, or secure with skewers.

Place the goose on a rack in a large roasting tin. Roast for 30 minutes. Reduce the oven temperature to gas 4/180°C/350°F. Roast for a further 3 hours 20 minutes, removing the fat from the tin at regular intervals.

To crisp the skin, 15 minutes before the goose is ready, sprinkle a little cold water over it. Test to see if the meat is cooked by sticking a sharp knife or skewer into the thigh. If the juice runs clear the goose is cooked.

Remove the bird from the oven and carefully lift it on to a warmed serving dish. Pour the excess fat from the pan. Add 1 pint/ 2½ cups/600ml of giblet stock (bouillon) to the pan and mix with the goodness that has come from the bird. Boil to reduce and thicken and season to taste, adding ¼ pint/½ cup/150 ml dry cider.

Serve with the gravy, dumplings, and onion, apple or gooseberry sauce or spiced pears.

Apple Sauce

SERVES 6–8

*2 large cooking apples,
   peeled, cored and chopped*
4 fl oz/4 tbsp/100ml water
1oz/2 tbsp/25g butter
2 tbsp sugar
1 tsp lemon juice
pinch of salt

Michaelmas falls at the time of year when apples are beginning to fall and the windfalls have to be used quickly because of bruising. One way to use them up is to make a sauce to accompany the goose.

METHOD

Place the apples and water in a pan and cook on a gentle heat until the apples are soft and pulpy. Remove from the heat and rub the mixture through a fine wire sieve, or put through a blender or food processor.

Stir in the butter, sugar, lemon juice and salt and pour into a warmed sauceboat or jug.

Green Gooseberry Sauce

SERVES 6–8

*10oz/1²⁄₃ cups/275g fresh
   gooseberries*
*grated rind and juice of 1
   lemon*
*salt and freshly ground black
   pepper*
¹⁄₂oz/1 tbsp/15g butter
1 tsp caster sugar

This is another very good sauce for goose as its acidity helps to counteract the grease from the bird.

METHOD

Top and tail the gooseberries and put into a pan with the lemon juice and rind. Cover and toss over a low heat until the fruit is tender. Put through a wire sieve, or pulp in a blender or food processor to make a purée.

Season with salt and pepper and stir in the butter and sugar. Mix well and turn into a warmed sauceboat or jug.

Orange Sauce

SERVES 6–8

¹⁄₂ the bird's liver
1oz/2 tbsp/25g butter
1 small bay leaf
1 tbsp plain (cake) flour
*1 pint/2¹⁄₂ cups/600ml giblet
   or poultry stock (bouillon)*
*grated rind and juice of 2
   oranges*

Orange sauce is equally good with duck or turkey.

METHOD

Chop the liver finely, saving the blood. Heat the butter in a pan with the bay leaf and add the liver and blood. Simmer until browned.

Sprinkle in the flour and stir well together until smooth. Cook, stirring, for 2 minutes. Remove from the heat and gradually stir in the stock (bouillon), mixing carefully.

Add the grated orange rind, return to the heat and cook, stirring

salt and freshly ground black
  pepper
1–2 tbsp brandy

all the time, until the sauce thickens. Season to taste and add the orange juice. Cook for a further 2–3 minutes. Just before serving stir in the brandy.

Onion Sauce

SERVES 6–8

4 medium onions, or 4
  bunches of spring onions
  (scallions) peeled and
  chopped
¼ pint/½ cup/150ml water
¼ pint/½ cup/150ml milk
1 slice turnip, approximately
  1 inch/2.5 cm thick
2oz/4 tbsp/50g butter
2 tsp grated nutmeg
½ tsp salt
¼ tsp freshly ground black
  pepper
2 fl oz/4 tbsp/50ml single
  (light) cream

At Michaelmas scallion onions were ready, and as they have to be used quickly they were ideal for the sauce to serve with the goose, and were excellent for sage and onion stuffing. This recipe can be made with either scallions or large onions.

METHOD

Place the onions, water, milk and turnip into a pan and bring to the boil. Simmer for 20 minutes until soft and beginning to pulp.

Remove the pan from the heat and add the butter, nutmeg, salt and pepper. Mash the mixture with a wooden spoon, or put through a blender or food processor, to make a smooth sauce.

Add the cream and mix thoroughly. Serve in a warmed sauceboat or jug.

Apple, Onion and Sage Stuffing

SERVES 6–8

2 medium cooking apples,
  peeled and grated
2 small onions, chopped
8 fresh sage leaves, chopped
8 pickled walnuts, cut into
  quarters
8oz/2 cups/225g fresh white
  breadcrumbs
2 beaten eggs
salt and freshly ground black
  pepper
grated rind and juice of 1
  lemon

This is an alternative recipe for a stuffing for the goose, sent to me by Jenny Marsland from Sark in the Channel Islands.

METHOD

Mix all the ingredients together and stuff into the cavity of the bird. Sew up the opening securely or secure with skewers.

Dumplings

ENOUGH FOR 5–6 PEOPLE

4oz/1 cup/100g plain (cake)
*   flour*
1¹/₂oz/just over ¹/₄ cup/40g
*   shredded suet*
1 tbsp chopped fresh parsley
¹/₂ tsp mixed dried herbs
¹/₂ tsp salt
¹/₄ tsp baking powder
freshly ground black pepper
a little water

Mix all together and bind with enough water to give a stiff mixture. Divide into 12 balls. Drop into boiling water and simmer for 40 minutes or roast in a little fat (shortening) for 40 minutes.

Barnstaple Fair Pears

SERVES 6

2lb/900g pears, peeled, cored
*   and halved*
cold water
1lb/450g soft brown or
*   demerara sugar*
grated rind and juice of 1
*   lemon*
1 wineglass of port or claret
5–6 cloves
a few drops of cochineal
whole blanched almonds

Barnstaple fair was held in the middle of September, starting with a ceremony at the Guildhall, and lasted for three days. Special foods on sale there included spiced ale, toast soaked in ale, cheese, gingerbreads and apple tarts. The custom at festive times in Devon was to make a large apple pie filled to the brim with good baking apples, sugar and lemon. Just before serving the pastry was lifted up and a quart of piping hot spiced ale was poured in. The same sort of pie was made in Bedfordshire at Christmas and was called Florentine apple pie.

These spiced pears were generally served in private houses and restaurants at fair time.

METHOD

Put the pears into a pan with enough cold water to barely cover them. Add the sugar, the lemon rind and juice, the wine or port and the cloves.

Simmer gently until soft. Remove from the heat and add the cochineal.

When cold lay in a serving dish and push the almonds into the fruit so that they stand upright. Serve cold with Devonshire clotted cream or double (whipping) cream.

Spiced Pears

SERVES 6–8

½ cinnamon stick
2 tsp whole allspice
8 cloves
12oz/1½ cups/350g
*   granulated sugar*
½ pint/1¼ cups/300ml
*   white wine vinegar*
2lb/900g dessert pears

This is an ideal dish to serve with goose since it offers an opportunity to use windfalls or freshly picked fruit, and offers a delicious alternative to apple sauce.

Prepare the pears at least one day before needed so that all the flavours soak into the fruit. Keep covered in the refrigerator and then warm gently through.

METHOD

Tie the cinnamon stick, allspice and cloves into a little muslin bag. Put the sugar, vinegar and spices into a pan. Stir over a gentle heat until the sugar dissolves.

Peel, core and cut each pear into 8 slices. Add to the pan and simmer until tender. Remove the pears to a dish and boil the sauce quickly to reduce and thicken it. Pour over the pears and chill until needed.

Brandy Snaps

**MAKES APPROXIMATELY
10–12 BISCUITS**

2oz/4 tbsp/50g butter
2oz/½ cup/50g plain (cake)
*   flour*
½ tsp ground ginger
2oz/just over ¼ cup/50g
*   demerara sugar*
2oz/1½ tbsp/50g golden
*   syrup*
½ tsp lemon juice
a few drops of vanilla essence
*   (extract)*

The most famous brandy snaps come from the Cotswold hiring fairs, and are descendants of 'gauffres' or wafers dating back to the twelfth century or earlier. These were made by pouring a fine batter into special wafer irons that stamped a design on to both sides of the cake. The brandy snaps are very similar in texture and flavour to other wakes cakes and fairings, but are rolled round wooden spoon handles and then, when cold and set, filled with whipped cream.

METHOD

Preheat the oven to gas 4/180°C/350°F. Grease 2 large baking trays.

Put the butter, flour, ginger, sugar and syrup into a pan and boil for 2 minutes. Mix in the lemon juice and vanilla essence (extract).

Spoon the mixture in 10–12 rounds on to the prepared trays, leaving plenty of space in between. Bake for 10–12 minutes until golden and perforated.

Remove from the oven and allow to cool for 2 minutes, then curl quickly round wooden spoon handles or shape into cones. Leave to cool completely then fill with whipped cream.

Potato dishes

Potatoes form the basis for all sorts of Hallowe'en dishes in both Scotland and Ireland. Introduced into Ireland in the 1590s, by the 1800s they were the staple diet in rural areas. They are still cooked in all sorts of unusual ways to make dishes which often have rather colourful names.

Champ (in Scotland called champit tatties) is a simple dish of mashed potatoes mixed with spring onions, milk and butter. Colcannon, a favourite in Scotland and Ireland, is similar to champ, but the potatoes are mixed with cabbage and onion. In Scotland it also includes mashed carrots and turnips. In spring a similar dish was served with nettle tops and other health-giving herbs. In some Irish households the colcannon was served in a large communal dish around which the family sat, each with a spoon. A hollow was made in the middle of the colcannon and a large piece of butter was dropped in. This melted with the heat of the potatoes, and the idea was to dip your spoon into the butter and then into the potato mixture. On 31 October the hearth was swept and a dish of colcannon left out for the *daoine si* (the good people), who show their gratitude by helping to bring good luck to the household in the coming year.

Potato or 'tattie' cakes for Hallowe'en were made by making little cakes of raw grated potatoes, flour, milk and eggs, and baking them on the griddle. When milk and salt were added to the mixture they were sometimes eaten instead of bread, and called 'dippity'. 'Stampy' cakes were similar but had caraway seeds and cream added, and 'boxty' was made by mixing mashed cooked potatoes with grated raw potatoes and flour. This was then cooked as pancakes, bread or dumplings. Boxty is probably one of Ireland's most celebrated

Hallowe'en dishes and appears in several verses of the following nature:

Boxty on the griddle,
Boxty on the pan.
If you don't eat boxty
You'll never get a man.

A silver sixpence was usually wrapped in greaseproof paper and hidden in the colcannon, champ or boxty dishes before serving. To find it meant good luck in the coming year.

Boxty Pancakes

These are what are referred to in the poem as 'boxty on the pan'.

SERVES 6

½lb/225g raw potatoes
½lb/225g cooked, mashed potatoes
8oz/2 cups/25g plain (cake) flour
1 tsp salt
buttermilk or skimmed milk
a little oil or lard for frying

METHOD

Wash and peel the raw potatoes and grate them into a linen cloth. Wring them out lightly, catching the liquid in a basin. Put the potatoes from the cloth into another basin and mix with the cooked mashed potatoes.

Leave the liquid from the grated potatoes in the basin until the starchy sediment settles and the water on the top is clear. Pour off the water and add the starch to the potato mixture. Add the flour and salt and mix well.

Make a well in the middle and add enough buttermilk or milk to give a batter of dropping consistency. Beat well until thoroughly mixed. Leave for a few minutes before frying.

Heat a griddle or heavy frying pan (skillet) and grease with a little oil or lard. Drop spoonfuls of the batter on to the hot pan and move the pan around so that the batter spreads evenly.

When the pancake is browned underneath, turn and brown the other side. When cooked, spread with butter. Keep hot in oven until ready to serve sprinkled with sugar.

Champ

SERVES 4

8 medium potatoes, peeled
8–10 spring onions
¼ pint/½ cup/150ml milk
salt and freshly ground black
   pepper
2oz/4 tbsp/50g butter

Cook the potatoes so that they are soft but not mushy, then drain and mash them. Keep hot.

Chop the spring onions finely and boil them in the milk for 5 minutes. Add this to the potatoes and beat thoroughly until smooth, fluffy and white. Season to taste, make a hollow in the top and serve with the butter melting in the hollow.

Potato Pudding

SERVES 6

2lb/900g potatoes, boiled,
   drained and mashed
12oz/3 cups/350g plain
   (cake) flour
salt and freshly ground black
   pepper
a large pinch of ground
   allspice
½ cup milk
1oz/2 tbsp/25g butter

This is another Irish favourite for Hallowe'en, and like the other dishes often had a ring hidden in it before serving. It is eaten like champ and colcannon with a generous lump of butter in a hollow on top. Because the potato pudding is cooked very slowly the starch in the potatoes acquires a sweet flavour, and sometimes apples, spice, caraway seeds, eggs and sugar are added and the pudding is eaten after the main course as a dessert rather than as part of the savoury course.

Potato pudding was also a favourite in Wales as an accompaniment to roast goose.

METHOD

Preheat the oven to gas 2/150°C/300°F. Grease a large casserole or pie dish with butter.

Mix the mashed potato with the flour, salt, pepper, allspice and milk. Pile the potato mixture into the prepared dish.

Cover and bake for 4 hours – it needs this long for the potatoes to become sweet in flavour.

Mash of Nine Sorts
(*Stwmp Naw Rhyw*)

SERVES 6

6 medium potatoes, peeled
and cut into fairly small
pieces
4 carrots, peeled and sliced
4 turnips, peeled and sliced
4 parsnips, peeled and sliced
1lb/450g peas
1oz/2 tbsp/25g butter
2 leeks, cleaned and cut into
thin slices
salt and freshly ground black
pepper
a little milk

This is a Welsh dish for Hallowe'en, similar to colcannon and champ but using nine ingredients. Like the Irish and Scottish dishes, this was usually served in a communal dish and each person would dip into it, and a wedding ring was concealed in the mixture. Another favourite was *punch nep*, made with turnips and potatoes mashed together, beaten with butter and served with pies and meat dishes.

METHOD

Boil the potatoes, carrots, turnips and parsnips together in salted water until soft but not mushy. Drain and mash.

Boil the peas in a little salted water until just cooked. Drain.

Melt the butter in a frying pan (skillet) and fry the leeks until soft but not brown.

Mix all the vegetables together. Add the salt and pepper and a little milk and blend well so that all the ingredients are evenly distributed. Serve immediately.

Colcannon

SERVES 4

8 medium potatoes, peeled
approximately 8oz/225g
cooked white cabbage
salt and freshly ground black
pepper
a little milk
1 onion, peeled and chopped
oil or dripping for frying
2oz/4 tbsp/50g butter

Cook the potatoes until they are soft but not mushy. Drain and mash. Chop the cabbage and add to the potatoes with salt and pepper and a little milk. Mix thoroughly.

Heat the oil or dripping in a frying pan (skillet) and fry the onion until transparent and just turning golden brown. Add the potato mixture to the pan, mix it with the onion and fry until brown.

Cut the mixture roughly, turn and continue cooking until there are lots of brown, crisp pieces. To divine who of your guests will be the first to wed, wrap a wedding ring in plenty of greaseproof paper and slip it into the mixture.

Make a hollow on the top and serve piping hot with a large knob of butter melting in the hollow.

Gingerbreads and Parkins

The custom of eating gingerbreads and parkins at Hallowe'en seems to derive from the pagan practice of baking special cakes to celebrate the first day of winter. These cakes were generally made of oatmeal, and later treacle (molasses), ginger and other spices were added. In Lancashire the cakes were called Harcakes after the god Har (one of the names for Odin) and in Derbyshire they were Thor cakes after the Scandinavian god of thunder, war and agriculture. Today gingerbreads and parkins are closely associated with Guy Fawkes Night on 5 November.

In the days of cooking on open fires, parkin was baked directly on a bakestone or hearthstone, and was consequently sometimes called 'tharve cake' from 'the hearth cake'. Eighteenth-century gingerbreads were rather dryer than today's and were often standard fillers for children and workers as well as being a festive food. The plainer types, using dripping rather than butter, were cheaper to make.

These recipes for two gingerbreads and two parkins show how they vary around the country. The Essex recipe from 1915 adds caraway seeds as well as a glass of brandy.

Essex Gingerbread

MAKES 1 × 8 INCH/20 CM SQUARE CAKE

8oz/1 cup/225g butter, softened

8oz/1 cup/225g sugar

10oz/6½ tbsp/275g black treacle (molasses), slightly warmed

12oz/3 cups/350g plain (cake) flour

2 tsp baking powder

6 tsp ground ginger

1 tsp grated nutmeg

3–4 tsp caraway seeds

1 glass brandy

This makes a really gooey, delicious, dark cake. If preferred, the caraway seeds may be left out and replaced with raisins, candied chopped peel or chopped crystallized ginger.

METHOD

Preheat the oven to gas 3/170°C/325°F. Grease and line an 8 inch/ 20 cm square tin.

Beat together the sugar and butter until light and fluffy. Add the treacle (molasses) and beat again. Work in the flour, baking powder, ginger, nutmeg and caraway seeds until evenly distributed. Finally stir in the brandy.

Turn into the prepared tin and bake for 1¾–2 hours.

Cartmel Gingerbread

MAKES 1 × 8 INCH/20 CM SQUARE CAKE

8oz/1 cup/225g margarine
2 tbsp black treacle (molasses)
8oz/1 cup/225g granulated sugar
1lb/4 cups/450g self-raising (all-purpose) flour
1 heaped tsp ground ginger
2 eggs, beaten
2–3 tsp demerara sugar
chopped candied peel etc. (optional)

This recipe was given to me by Nan Murphy, who first came across it in Cartmel in the Lake District. She says it is a very easy, cheap cake that is an excellent stand-by for hungry mouths. It keeps well and freezes very successfully (if you can resist eating it as soon as it's baked).

METHOD

Preheat the oven to gas 3/170°C/325°F. Grease an 8 inch/20 cm square tin.

Gently melt the margarine and add the treacle (molasses), sugar, flour and ginger. Mix well. Add the beaten eggs and if necessary a little water or milk to give a floppy, wet consistency.

If liked, add some chopped, candied peel, or chopped stem ginger, or a few raisins, sultanas or nuts. Turn the mixture into the prepared tin and sprinkle the demerara sugar over the top.

Bake for 1 hour until a warm skewer comes out clean. Remove from the oven and leave to cool in the tin for 5 minutes before turning out on to a wire rack to cool completely.

Westmorland Parkin

MAKES 16–20 PIECES

8oz/1 cup/225g butter
1lb/10½ tbsp/450g black treacle (molasses)
1lb/3 cups/450g fine oatmeal
8oz/2 cups/225g plain (cake) flour
1 tsp ground allspice
2 tsp baking powder
8oz/1¼ cups/225g demerara sugar
1 tsp salt
1 tsp bicarbonate of soda
½ cup milk

This recipe was sent to me by Alice Taylor of Underbarrow in Cumbria.

METHOD

Preheat the oven to gas 5/190°C/375°F. Grease a large, shallow meat tin. Melt the butter and treacle (molasses) together. Sift the flour with the allspice and baking powder and mix with the sugar and salt.

Pour the treacle (molasses) and butter and mix well until all the ingredients are evenly distributed. Dissolve the bicarbonate of soda in the milk and add to the mixture. Mix thoroughly.

Pour into the prepared tin and cook for 1½–2 hours. Remove from the oven and leave to cool in the tin.

When cold cut into squares.

Yorkshire Parkin

MAKES 12–16 PIECES

4oz/½ cup/100g butter,
    softened
8oz/2 cups/225g plain (cake)
    flour
8oz/just over 1½ cups/225g
    medium oatmeal
4oz/½ cup/100g sugar
pinch of salt
1 tsp ground ginger
2 tsp bicarbonate of soda
1oz/1 tbsp/25g mixed candied
    peel
8oz/5½ tbsp/225g black
    treacle (molasses)
1 egg, beaten
¼ pint/½ cup/150ml milk

Preheat the oven to gas 3/150°C/300°F. Grease and line a tin 10 inches × 7 inches/25 × 15 cm or 8 inches/20 cm square.

Rub the butter into the flour then mix in the oatmeal, sugar, salt, ginger, bicarbonate of soda and peel. Mix well together.

Mix together the treacle (molasses), egg and milk and blend with the dry ingredients to give a soft consistency. Turn into the prepared tin and bake for 1–1¼ hours until a warm skewer comes out clean.

Remove from the oven, cool in the tin for 10–15 minutes then turn out on to a wire rack to cool completely. When cold, store in an airtight container for 2–3 days then cut into squares.

Apples for Hallowe'en

Apples have been associated with Hallowe'en customs for centuries. Games played at the celebrations also involve apples, favourites being apple bobbing and the apple and candle game. Apple bobbing (or apple ducking) involves trying to catch in the teeth apples bobbing in a barrel of water. To play the apple and candle game participants are blindfolded and have their hands tied behind their backs. They then try to catch with their teeth apples that are hanging on strings from a horizontal line or stick. To make the game more entertaining for the spectators, pieces of candle also hang from the line. These games have given their name to the evening and Hallowe'en is known in some places as Bob Apple or Duck Apple Night, and in Wales it is called Apple and Candle Night.

In Ireland, favourite Hallowe'en dishes include apple amber, apple dumplings and friars' omelette (*froise*, meaning cooked or fried in a batter). Because of the sizzling sound made when batter is dropped into hot fat, froisey or frausey came to mean a small jubilation or feast.

Toffee Apples

Toffee apples were popular at fairgrounds and for Hallowe'en. In the days before the general availability of sugar they were quite expensive. Only small ripe apples that have no bruises or blemishes should be used.

MAKES 10–12 APPLES

4oz/¹/₂ cup/100g butter
8oz/5¹/₂ tbsp/225g black treacle (molasses)
1lb/2 cups/450g brown sugar
1 tbsp vinegar
10–12 small apples

METHOD

Wash the apples, wipe dry and push a wooden stick into each, downwards through the core.

Mix the toffee ingredients together and boil for 20 minutes. Dip the apples in quickly and stand on a rack or on oiled greaseproof paper to set.

Apple Amber

SERVES 4–6

shortcrust pastry made with
8oz/2 cups/225g plain
(cake) flour (see page 132)
1lb/450g apples, peeled,
cored and sliced
3 tbsp brown sugar
2 tbsp water
1 tsp grated lemon rind
2 eggs, separated
1 tbsp caster sugar
1 tbsp icing (confectioner's)
sugar
1oz/¼ cup/25g shredded,
blanched almonds

First make the pastry as on page 132 and chill for 15 minutes.

Preheat the oven to gas 4/180°C/350°F. Grease a pie dish.

On a floured board, roll out the pastry to a thickness of approximately ⅛ inch /0.25 cm and use to line the pie dish.

Put the apples into a pan with the brown sugar, water and lemon rind. Cook, uncovered, until pulpy. Leave to cool, then beat in the egg yolks.

Turn into the pastry-lined dish and bake for 25–30 minutes.

Beat the egg whites until stiff and then beat in the caster and icing (confectioner's) sugars. Fold in the almonds and pile the mixture on top of the apples. Return to the oven, reduce the heat to gas 1/110°C/ 225°F, and cook for 30–40 minutes until the meringue is browned.

Apple Dumplings

SERVES 6

shortcrust pastry made with
1lb/4 cups/450g plain
(cake) flour (see page 132)
6 apples, peeled and cored
2oz/4 tbsp/50g butter or
margarine
2oz/4 tbsp/50g sugar
6 cloves
a little milk

In Ireland large apple dumplings, with a suet and flour crust, were commonly made. Seamus Duff, remembering his childhood in the *Journal of Larne and District Folklore Society* in 1982, wrote: 'I can still see the big round shape in the white cloth being lifted out of the boiling water and being dished out to us impatient youngsters while it was still too hot to eat. There were always a few threepenny bits scattered through it and the more we ate the better the chances of financial gain.'

METHOD

First make the pastry as on page 132 and chill for 15 minutes.

Preheat the oven to gas 6/200°C/400°F. Grease a baking tray.

On a floured board, roll out the pastry thinly and cut into 6 rounds.

Cream the butter and sugar together and fill the apples with the mixture. Add a clove to each apple. Place each apple on a pastry round.

Dampen the edges of the pastry with a little milk. Draw up the edges and press together. Pat into shape and place upside down on the prepared baking tray. Brush with milk and bake for 35 minutes (cooking time will depend on the size and ripeness of the apples).

Friars' Omelette

SERVES 4

FOR THE BATTER

1 egg yolk
8 fl oz/1 cup/225g milk
4oz/1 cup/100g plain (cake)
  flour
1 tbsp sugar
a pinch of mixed spice
1 egg white

2–3 good cooking apples,
  peeled, cored and sliced
2oz/4 tbsp/50g butter
sugar for dredging

First make the batter. Mix together the egg yolk, milk, flour, sugar and spice and beat hard for 2 minutes to incorporate plenty of air. Beat the egg white and fold in.

Heat the oven to gas 2/150°C/300°F. Warm a serving dish.

Melt the butter in a frying pan (skillet) and fry the apples gently until soft. Lift out and keep hot in the oven.

Pour a shallow covering of batter into the pan and cook over a moderate heat until set. Toss over and while the underside is browning lay some of the hot apples on top. Sprinkle with sugar and when the batter is cooked, fold over and lift on to the serving dish. Keep hot in the oven.

Repeat until all the batter and apples are used up. Serve with a little cider poured over and a good sprinkling of sugar.

Barm Brack

MAKES 1 × 8 INCH/20 CM
SQUARE CAKE

2oz/4 tbsp/50g butter,
  softened
1lb/4 cups/450g plain (cake)
  flour
1/2 tsp mixed spice
pinch of salt
3/4oz/1 1/2 tbsp/22g fresh yeast
2 tbsp caster sugar
1/2 pint/1 1/4 cups/300ml milk
2 eggs, beaten
1lb/3 cups/450g mixed dried
  fruit (raisins, sultanas,
  currants)
4oz/1/2 cup/100g mixed
  candied peel

This is an Irish speciality: barm means leaven or yeast, and brack means speckled, referring to the little dots of fruit that appear in the bread. The loaf is traditional for Hallowe'en, and as with most Hallowe'en dishes a ring is usually wrapped in paper or foil and hidden inside. Whoever gets the ring will be the first to marry.

Barm brack is also traditional for New Year celebrations and other festive occasions during the year.

METHOD

Grease an 8 inch/20 cm square tin. Rub or cut the butter into the flour. Add the spice and salt.

Cream the yeast with 1 tsp of the sugar. Add the rest of the sugar and mix well. Warm the milk slightly and add to the yeast with most of the beaten egg (keep a little back for glazing the top).

Beat the liquid into the flour mixture and blend to make a stiff, elastic dough. Fold in the dried fruit and peel and mix well. Turn into the prepared tin to half fill. Cover with a damp cloth and leave in a warm place to double in size.

Preheat the oven to Gas 6/200°C/400°F.

Brush the top with beaten egg and bake for 1 hour until a warm skewer comes out clean. Remove from the oven, turn out on to a wire rack and leave to cool.

Cloutie Dumpling

SERVES 12

*(half quantities are plenty for
a normal family-sized
pudding)*

*12oz/3 cups/350g self-raising
(all-purpose) flour*
12oz/1½ cups/350g sugar
4oz/½ cup/100g margarine
8oz/1½ cups/225g currants
8oz/1½ cups/225g raisins
2oz/⅓ cup/50g candied peel
1 tsp mixed spice
2 tsp ground cinnamon
pinch of salt
2 eggs, beaten
a little milk

This very filling pudding has always been a favourite in Scotland
and Ireland for Christmas and Hallowe'en. In the 1983/4 edition of
the *Journal of Larne and District Folklore Society*, Patricia McAllister
wrote of the careful preparations that took place to make the
pudding – the shopping for the dried fruit and flour, the washing
and drying of the fruit, the chopping of the suet, and the orange and
lemon peel. She tells how, after dinner, 'the baking resumed; the
currants, raisins and sultanas were dry by this time and were
gathered carefully and left beside the bake-board. The black pot
which had held the broth was washed, half filled with water,
. . . the flour bag to hold the dumpling was dropped into this and
the whole lot returned to the iron grid over the fire to boil.'

The pudding mixture was then made and 'the flour bag was taken
from the boiling water, wrung out, handfuls of flour were shaken into it and the surplus shaken out, the mixture in the bowl was emptied
into the prepared bag, tied tightly with a large piece of string and
the whole lot was lowered gently into the boiling water, the extra
piece of string being tied to the handle of the pot, and the long
wait began.'

After three hours or so of boiling, the dumpling was turned out
on to an enamel plate and set in front of the fire to dry. 'There it sat in
all its splendour – the pinky skin turning to a rich brown as the heat
from the glowing fire slowly dried it out, the steam rising from it
like an offering to the gods. The raisins and sultanas plumped out by

the long boiling shining all over its surface and the lovely smell of the spices and fruit filled the room.' It was served in soup plates and covered with thick, creamy custard.

METHOD

Grease a large pudding bowl or, if using a cloth, sprinkle the inside liberally with flour.

Mix together all the dry ingredients. Add the eggs and milk and mix well to a scone-like mixture. Make sure that all the ingredients are evenly distributed.

Turn into the pudding bowl or cloth. If using a bowl, cover with a piece of greased paper and tie a cloth over the top, securing tightly with a piece of string. If using a bag, tie the neck tightly with a piece of string. Steam or boil for 3–3½ hours.

St Clement's Day Rice Pudding

SERVES 4–5

3oz/½ cup/75g pudding rice
3oz/just under ½ cup/75g demerara sugar
½ pint/1¼ cups/300ml single (light) cream
½ pint/1¼ cups/300ml milk
1oz/2 tbsp/25g butter
2 egg yolks, beaten
½ tsp grated nutmeg
pinch of salt
4 egg whites
4 tbsp caster sugar

St Clement's Day falls on 23 November, but in the old Julian calendar that was used in Scotland until 1600 and in England until 1752, the feast day was celebrated on 4 December. In Essex, little clementy cakes were baked, much the same as cattern cakes (see page 100), and made from a piece of bread dough with spices, dried fruit and sugar added to make it special. In Cambridge, bakers would always share a communal meal, and at Tenby in Wales, boat owners provided a large meal of roast goose and rice pudding for their crews.

Everyday rice pudding was made special for festive occasions, such as St Clement's Day, by adding a meringue topping as with this recipe, or by adding butter, fine suet or marrow-fat to make it rich and creamy. In medieval days almond milk was used. This was made by pounding together sweet and bitter almonds, then adding water and sugar, and boiling to make a thick creamy fluid.

METHOD

Preheat the oven to gas 3/170°C/325°F. Grease a pie dish. Place the rice in the dish and add the sugar, cream, milk, butter, beaten egg yolks, nutmeg and salt. Stir and bake for 2 hours.

Whisk the egg whites until stiff and fold in the caster sugar. Pile on top of the rice, increase the oven temperature to gas 4/180°C/350°F and bake for a further 30 minutes until the top of the meringue is golden.

Cattern Cakes (1)

**MAKES APPROXIMATELY
24–26 CAKES**

½oz/½ tsp/15g fresh yeast

½ tsp caster sugar

*¾ pint/just under 1 pint/
    450ml warm water*

*1lb/450g plain (cake) flour,
    and plenty more for flouring
    the board and hands*

1 tsp salt

*1oz/2 tbsp/25g butter,
    softened*

*2–3oz/4–6 tbsp/50–75g
    caster sugar*

1 egg, beaten

*a few caraway seeds or
    currants*

Recipes for cattern cakes, made for St Catherine's Day, the lace-makers' holiday on 25 November, vary enormously. Some are very simple, others are quite rich and elaborate. Mary Boyd, a Bedfordshire lace-maker, wrote to me to say, 'the only cattern cake I have eaten was a small bun made with yeast, containing caraway seeds and a small amount of lemon peel'. She says that she thinks it very unlikely that lace-makers, who were poor, could have afforded the currants, ground almonds, sugar, eggs and butter needed for some recipes. She goes on, 'It was more the custom to set aside a piece of their normal bread dough and add maybe the seeds, peel and a little sugar.' More elaborate recipes have probably evolved as people could afford more expensive ingredients.

Similar cakes called tanders were made a few days later for the feast day of St Andrew, the true patron saint of lace-makers, on 30 November. A piece of bread dough was again set aside and mixed with spices and caraway seeds to give cakes that were a little more special than ordinary bread.

This is a traditional simple recipe for cattern cakes. It is quite a long operation to make these and the dough is very sticky and wet. The more modern cattern cakes on page 101 are easier, but these are more authentic.

METHOD

Cream the yeast and sugar together and pour into the warm water. Blend thoroughly. Sift the flour and salt and make a well in the middle. Pour in the yeast mixture and sprinkle a little flour over the top. Do not mix.

Stand the bowl in a warm place for about 20 minutes, then mix with a fork to an elastic dough, adding a little more warm water if necessary. With well-floured hands knead well until the dough comes cleanly away from the sides of the bowl.

On a well-floured board, knead the dough with the butter, sugar, egg and seeds or currants. Place the mixture in a clean bowl and cover with a damp cloth. Leave in a warm place for 2 hours.

Preheat the oven to gas 4/180°C/350°F. Grease 2 baking trays.

Form the dough into little buns and place well apart on the prepared trays. Leave in a warm place for about 20 minutes then bake for 15–20 minutes until lightly browned.

Cattern Cakes (2)

**MAKES APPROXIMATELY
16 CAKES**

*6oz/³⁄₄ cup/175g butter,
    softened*
6oz/ ⁷⁄₈ cup/175g caster sugar
*8oz/2 cups/225g plain (cake)
    flour*
1 tsp baking powder
large pinch of mixed spice
*3oz/1 cup/75g ground
    almonds*
1 egg, beaten
4oz/²⁄₃ cup/75g currants

A more modern recipe, sent to me by Anne Biley of Northampton.

METHOD

Preheat the oven to gas 6/200°C/400°F. Grease a large baking tray.

Cream the butter and sugar together until light and fluffy. Sift together the flour, baking powder and spice. Stir in the ground almonds. Fold the flour mixture into the creamed butter and sugar and add enough beaten egg to make a stiff dough.

On a lightly floured board roll out the dough to a rectangle about ³⁄₈ inch/just under 1cm thick, 8 inches/20 cm wide and 12 inches/ 30 cm long. Sprinkle the currants over the dough and roll up like a swiss roll, being careful not to allow the dough to break. Dampen the edges and seal.

Cut into slices about ½ inch/1 cm thick and lay the slices flat on the prepared trays. Bake for 15 minutes until pale golden.

Remove from the oven and leave to cool for 2–3 minutes on the tray before removing to a wire rack to cool completely.

Minced Collops

SERVES 4

1 tbsp dripping or oil
*1 medium onion, peeled and
    finely chopped*
*1lb/450g minced (ground)
    steak*
1 cup stock (bouillon)
*salt and freshly ground black
    pepper*
2–3 tsp oatmeal or barley
*1 tbsp mushroom ketchup
    (catsup)*

This traditional Scottish dish, often cooked for festive meals on St Andrew's Day on 30 November, is usually made with minced (ground) steak but can also be prepared with veal, hare or venison. At Andermas (also called Andry's day or Androiss Mess) the men and boys would go 'andra-ing' through the woods and fields to catch rabbits, squirrels and birds for the midday feast. The rest of the day was spent eating, drinking and having a merry time.

METHOD

Heat the dripping or oil in a frying pan (skillet) and cook the onion until transparent but not brown. Add the meat and brown carefully, breaking up the lumps with a wooden spoon until brown all over.

Add the stock, salt and pepper, mix well and simmer, for 1–1½ hours. Add the oatmeal or barley and the mushroom ketchup (catsup), mix and continue cooking for about 15–20 minutes until the oatmeal or barley is softened.

Serve on a warmed meat dish with mashed potato, fried bread or toast and garnished with slices of hard-boiled egg.

Cattern Cakes

RECIPE ON PAGE 100

Kingdom of Fife Pie

SERVES 7–8

rough puff pastry made with
8oz/2 cups/225g plain
(cake) flour (see page 133)
1 rabbit, cut into joints
forcemeat balls as below
1lb/450g pickled pork
2 hard-boiled eggs, sliced
½ tsp grated nutmeg
salt and freshly ground black
pepper
3 tbsp white wine
1 cup gravy or stock
(bouillon)

FOR THE FORCEMEAT BALLS

the rabbit's liver, chopped
4oz/1 cup/100g fresh
breadcrumbs
3 medium bacon rashers, cut
into small pieces
2 tbsp chopped fresh parsley
salt and pepper
grated rind of ½ lemon
1 tsp dried thyme
½ tsp nutmeg
1 egg, beaten

A traditional Scottish recipe often cooked for St Andrew's Day on 30 November. Haggis has always been one of the traditional dishes for this saint's day, other popular ones being singed sheep's head, sheep's head broth, minced collops (minced (ground) beef fried with breadcrumbs and oatmeal), roast goose and salt cod with egg sauce.

METHOD

Make the pastry as on page 133 and leave to chill for at least 30 minutes.

Put the rabbit joints into cold water and soak for an hour. Boil the innards and any bones to make stock (bouillon).

Preheat the oven to gas 7/220°C/425°F.

Make the forcemeat balls by mixing all the ingredients together so that all are evenly distributed, and shape into small balls the size of walnuts.

Slice the pickled pork.

Pack the rabbit joints, forcemeat balls, pork and eggs into an ovenproof dish. Sprinkle over the nutmeg, salt and pepper. Pour over the wine and ¾ of the stock (bouillon).

On a floured board, roll out the pastry to make a lid and use to cover the meats. Press the edges down firmly. Brush the top with beaten egg and make three slits in the top.

Bake for 15 minutes then reduce the heat to gas 4/180°C/350°F and bake for a further 1½–1¾ hours.

Before serving, add the remaining stock (bouillon) through the slits in the pastry.

Serve hot or cold.

Salt Cod with Egg Sauce

SERVES 4

1½lb/700g salt cod
2 tbsp chopped fresh parsley
1 cup vinegar

FOR THE SAUCE

6 hard-boiled eggs
4oz/½ cup/100g unsalted
  butter
freshly ground black pepper
pinch of mace

An anonymous English visitor to Edinburgh at the end of the eighteenth century noted: 'Cod-fish salted for a short time and not dried in the manner of common salt fish, and boiled with parsley and horseradish. They eat it with egg sauce, and it is extremely luscious and palatable.' This dish was sometimes called cabbie-claw and was served with parsnips, either plain boiled or puréed with a little cream and butter.

METHOD

Soak the fish in cold water, with a cupful of vinegar added, for 12 hours or overnight to draw out some of the salt. If the fish is very salty, change the water every 3–4 hours.

Place the fish in a saucepan and barely cover with fresh cold water. Bring to the boil and cook gently for 20 minutes or until the fish begins to fall away from the bones.

Meanwhile, heat the oven to gas 2/150°C/300°F. Warm a serving dish. Drain the fish, remove any skin and bones, and flake carefully. Place on the serving dish and scatter the parsley over the top. Keep hot in the oven.

To make the sauce, separate the egg whites from the yolks and chop the whites roughly. Add the yolks and chop both together but not too small. Place in a small pan with the butter and bring gently to the boil. Add the pepper and mace, stir well and pour over the fish. Serve immediately.

Scots Marmalade Pudding

SERVES 6

1–2 tbsp raisins
6oz/1½ cups/175g fresh
  breadcrumbs
2½ cups milk
3 eggs, separated
3oz/½ cup/75g soft brown
  sugar
2 tbsp thick marmalade

This was one of the favourite puddings for special meals on St Andrew's Day or at other times of national celebration. Other popular sweet dishes were Apple Puddings in Skins (a mixture of apples, grated biscuits, suet, cinnamon, nutmeg, wine or liqueur and sugar stuffed into the apple skins and baked or boiled), Prune or Apple Flory (fruit cooked with port or spices and covered with puff pastry) and Plum Pudding served with a wine and rum sauce.

METHOD

Grease a 2 pint/1.1 litre pudding basin. Scatter the raisins in the base.

Bring the milk to the boil and pour over the breadcrumbs. Leave to stand until almost cold. Beat the egg yolks with the sugar and stir into the cooled milk and bread mixture with the marmalade. Whisk the egg whites until very stiff and fold carefully in.

Pour the mixture into the prepared basin and cover. Stand the basin in a pan of boiling water that comes well up the sides of the basin and simmer for 1¾ hours.

Oatmeal Posset

SERVES 4

1 pint/2½ cups/1.1 litre milk
½ tsp grated nutmeg
½ tsp ground cinnamon
2 tbsp fine oatmeal
3 tbsp sweet white wine
3 tbsp ale
2 tbsp sugar

This thick, hot drink was often served as part of celebratory meals in Scotland and was another favourite for St Andrew's Day.

METHOD

Mix together the milk, nutmeg, cinnamon and oatmeal and bring to the boil. Boil for about 10 minutes until the oatmeal begins to soften.

In a small pan mix together the wine, ale and sugar and bring almost to the boil. Add to the milk and stir well. Simmer gently for 1–2 minutes then pour into a serving bowl and serve immediately.

Christmas Pudding

RECIPE ON PAGE 116

WINTER

In 1600 in Scotland and 1752 in England there was a major calendar change, from the Julian to the Gregorian calendar: as a result Christmas moved back by twelve days and the new year started on 1 January. For many years 6 January was known as Old Christmas Day, and 17 January as Old Twelfth Night, and the foods and festivities associated with these moveable feasts have inevitably become rather confused.

Christmas is, of course, the most important celebration of the Christian year, but the rituals and festivities we associate with the Christian festival probably developed from pagan Celtic celebrations of the winter solstice on 21 December. The pagan rituals involved a ceremonial cutting of mistletoe and the bringing into the house of evergreens, such as holly, in order to keep away evil spirits, and as a symbol of the continuation of life through the winter. A gruel, which much later developed into Christmas pudding, was served to represent a sort of Celtic cornucopia and a symbol of future abundance. From those early days onwards this season has always involved feasting on all sorts of special foods.

In medieval times a dressed boar's head, formerly a Celtic sacred dish throughout northern Europe, was served with frumenty. Later, goose and other fowl and game birds became the most popular dishes for Christmas dinner. The countryside was alive with game, including many breeds of bird now extinct, so there was plenty of choice. Poorer people throughout Britain would try to have something special for the main meal, and in large mansions enormous feasts were laid out for family, relatives, tenants, resident craftsmen, servants and friends. Elaborate dishes were prepared: goose stuffed with herbs, garlic, pears and quince; boned goose stuffed with boiled tongue in pastry with mincemeat; and the traditional Christmas pie containing five or six birds of different sizes, boned and stuffed inside each other. Any gaps were filled with forcemeat, pieces of game, herbs, spices, hardboiled eggs, stock and butter. The pastry crust that enveloped it was not to be eaten, but acted merely as an airtight seal to protect the delicacies within. According to the nursery rhyme Jack Horner put his thumb into a Christmas pie and pulled out a plum. Indeed he did. As steward to the last abbot of Glastonbury during the reign of Henry VIII he was entrusted with delivering a Christmas pie from the abbot to the king in London.

During the journey he peeped into the pie and found not the traditional meat filling but the deeds to several houses in Somerset. He helped himself to the deeds of the Manor of Mells.

In Ireland it was the tradition to start the festive season by eating parley cakes, made from flour and potatoes, on Christmas Eve; and at the same time on the Isle of Arran salt fish was always served with white sauce. In most of Britain until the end of the nineteenth century a goose was roasted and served on Christmas Day with a dish of spiced beef. While the goose was cooking and the women were preparing the meal, the men and boys worked up an appetite by playing a game of shinty (a type of hurling) in a nearby field; when they returned to their respective families, the man of the house was presented with the first mug of goose soup. In Yorkshire jugged hare was a favourite Christmas dish, and in the poorer areas of the north of England bullock's heart was sometimes served instead of goose. In Suffolk a cold rabbit pie was sometimes eaten, and in Cornwall, where pies were served at all festive occasions, giblet pie was the popular dish. Turkey has gradually taken over from goose as the main dish. Introduced to Europe from Mexico in the early sixteenth century, turkeys reached England by way of Levantine or Turkish merchants. As the English had difficulty with the Mexican name 'uexolotl', they named the bird after the merchants who introduced it.

Other Christmas dishes were prepared some weeks before. In many counties 'Advent' Sunday, which falls on or near 25 November, was the day for mixing the pudding, cake and mincemeat. The Christmas pudding mixture also has its origins in pagan days, when a thin porridge or pottage made with cornmeal or oats was served at the winter solstice festival. The pudding always took pride of place on the table, decorated with a sprig of holly to ward off evil spirits. The silver charms or coins traditionally hidden inside the pudding probably derive from the pea or bean inside a special cake made for Twelfth Night celebrations. This was a rich fruit cake, iced and decorated, and later adopted as Christmas cake. While some mention that, like decorated Christmas trees and Christmas cards, this sort of cake was introduced from Germany by Prince Albert, the rich Twelfth cake and decorated marzipan sweetmeats were Christmas specialities long before Victorian days.

Mince pies as we know them are a relatively modern sweet development of the Christmas pie. Some savoury pies were made with lamb or beef mixed with all sorts of spices and flavourings, dried and fresh fruits and fruit juices. Over the years the meat content slowly disappeared and the mixture gradually became the sweet mincemeat that we eat today, the only remnants of meat being the beef suet that most recipes include.

In many counties gingerbread, pepper cakes and yule breads were cooked to offer to visitors or carol singers. In Northumberland the gingerbread used to be shaped as men and dolls to symbolize the baby Jesus. Frumenty was a favourite breakfast dish, served with honey or sugar, milk and dried fruits, and a bowlful was often left outside the door at night for the fairies. In Whitby, Yorkshire, it was served on Christmas Eve with gingerbread and cheese. In areas of Britain where the Celtic influence is still strong – Scotland, Ireland, parts of Wales and the Isle of Man – Christmas is overshadowed by New Year celebrations. Here there are still special foods, songs, drinks and activities that do not exist in England.

In Scotland Hogmanay is still considered to be a very magical and significant celebration. Important preparations take place each year. A large joint of meat is cooked – either a piece of lamb or a haunch of venison – and left to cool, to be served in slices on New Year's Day with oatcakes and butter; or sometimes a hot haggis is eaten with clapshot, a mixture of mashed turnips and potatoes. Shortbread is also baked ready, using only the very best ingredients to ensure a fine, light, buttery cake. A huge cloutie dumpling (see page 98) is put to boil for hours in a pot on the stove. This was an ideal pudding for the evening of New Year's Eve, as it would sustain people through the long night of festivities. Leftovers would be fried the next day with bacon and served for breakfast. Special drinks are prepared meanwhile and set ready for the evening's celebrations. During the festivities whisky is often drunk from a communal glass, taken round the gathering by one of the men who fills the glass for each guest and offers the season's greetings. The festive cake is a black bun or party cake, much darker and richer than the southern Christmas cake.

In Ireland a large barm brack is baked (see page 97), which the man of the house, having taken three bites, proceeds to dash it against the door of the house in the name of the Trinity. What is left of the cake is then gathered up and eaten by the other members of the family. In the north of England, New Year's Eve was the day to visit friends and exchange gifts of pieces of cake and thick slices of bacon.

The south of England, by contrast, has very few special dishes for New Year's Eve or Day, although most families bake or buy shortbread. In Cambridgeshire beef in beer was a popular dish: the old ox that had been kept to work through the winter would be killed for meat in December when most of the work was finished, and cooked slowly in beer which helped to tenderize it. In Coventry it was the custom for godchildren to visit their god-parents on New Year's Day to receive their blessing and a triangular pastry filled with spices and dried fruit called a Coventry God-cake. The triangular shape represented the Holy Trinity, and the cakes were also some-times made by godmothers to be eaten at christenings.

The celebration of Twelfth Night, also called Three Kings Night, dates back to Roman times when there were huge feasts and games of forfeits, plays, disguising and general merrymaking. Over the years the traditional Twelfth cake became the large decorated spice and fruit cake that was popular until late Victorian times.

All sorts of warming drinks were brewed for Christmas, New Year and Twelfth Night, the best-known being the wassail bowl. This mixture of spiced ale and apples was drunk at several festivities throughout the year, and at Christmas was carried from house to house by carol singers or wassailers.

The final celebrations of the Christmas and New Year period used to take place on Plough Monday, the first Monday after Twelfth Night. After two weeks of rest from farm work the plough was taken to the parish church to be blessed, and then the local farm lads, dressed in colourful costumes, would dance through the streets, dragging the plough behind them performing plays, singing and begging for money. Traditional foods for Plough Monday were sausage rolls, bread and cheese and cheesecakes that were tossed by the villagers lining the route to the plough lads who caught them in their aprons, to be eaten later with mulled ale and beer. The period between the hilarity of Plough Monday and the celebration of Easter was a lean time for all but the really wealthy. Food stocks were low and had to be used carefully until spring brought a fresh supply of vegetables and meat.

Chestnut Soup

Chestnuts have long been a Christmas favourite in England for stuffing the turkey, for cooking with Brussels sprouts and for making thick nourishing soup.

SERVES 8–10

2lb/900g chestnuts

4 pints/10 cups/2.2 litres chicken or veal stock (bouillon)

2 stalks of celery, washed and roughly chopped

2 medium onions, peeled and roughly chopped

3–4 carrots, peeled and roughly chopped

2 tbsp chopped fresh parsley

salt and freshly ground black pepper

½ tsp powdered mace

large pinch cayenne pepper

¾ pint/just under 1 pint/ 400ml single (light) cream

METHOD

Preheat the oven to gas 6/200°C/400°F.

Slit the skin of each chestnut on the curved surface and lay on the flat side in a roasting tin. Pour ½ pint/1¼ cups/300ml water into the tin and roast for 10 minutes.

Peel the chestnuts while still hot, and remove the inner skin. Place in a heavy saucepan. Cover with the stock (bouillon) and add the vegetables, parsley, salt and pepper, mace and cayenne pepper. Boil for about 45 minutes until tender.

Purée the soup by putting through a food processor or liquidizer, or by working through a wire sieve. Check the seasoning and boil for a further 15 minutes.

Just before serving add the cream; warm through but do not boil.

Roast Turkey

1 turkey
2 stuffings, one for the crop
  and one for the main body,
  from following recipes
2–3 slices of bacon

BASTING JUICES

4oz/½ cup/100g melted
  butter
¼ pint/½ cup/150ml dry
  white wine
juice of 2 oranges
2 cloves of garlic, minced
  (ground)
a little stock (bouillon)
salt and freshly ground black
  pepper

After their introduction to Europe from Mexico in the sixteenth century, turkeys were reared in great flocks in Norfolk and Suffolk, and just before Christmas would be driven to London, foraging on the wayside verges on the way. Turkey gradually replaced roast goose as the standard main course for Christmas dinner.

METHOD

Prepare and truss the bird. Make the chosen stuffings and use to fill the main body and the crop. Lay the bacon over the breast and fix in place with skewers or cocktail sticks.

Preheat the oven to gas 7/220°C/425°F. Mix together the ingredients for the basting juices and baste the turkey well. Roast for 15–20 minutes then reduce the oven to gas 4/180°C/350°F and cook until done, allowing 15 minutes per pound (450g) for a bird under 14 pounds (6.3kg), 12 minutes per pound for a bird over 14 pounds.

About 20 minutes before serving remove the bacon and allow the breast to brown. Serve with traditional accompaniments of chipolata sausages, bread sauce, cranberry sauce or celery sauce, bacon rolls, braised onions, Brussels sprouts and gravy.

Chestnut Stuffing

8oz/225g chestnuts
8oz/2 cups/225g fresh
  breadcrumbs
8oz/1 cup/225g butter,
  melted
1 egg, beaten
1 tsp grated nutmeg
salt and freshly ground black
  pepper
a little stock (bouillon)

Cut off the tops of the chestnuts and bake or roast for about 20 minutes. Remove the outer shell and the inner skins and place the nuts in a saucepan with ½ pint/1¼ cups/300ml water. Simmer for about 15–20 minutes until tender.

Purée the nuts in a food processor or rub through a strong wire sieve. Add all the other ingredients and mix well.

Lemon Forcemeat

*4oz/1 cup/100g fresh
    breadcrumbs
2oz/³⁄₈ cup/50g shredded suet
grated rind of 1 lemon
juice of ½ lemon
2–3 tbsp chopped fresh
    parsley
1 egg, beaten*

This recipe comes from Rosemary Holmes of Bowness-on-Windermere in Cumbria. She uses the forcemeat in the wishbone end of the turkey, and says it is also excellent in a chicken that is to be eaten cold or a shoulder of veal.

METHOD

Mix all the ingredients together so that all are evenly distributed.

Bacon and Herb Stuffing

*2oz/4 tbsp/50g butter
4oz/just over ½ cup/100g
    smoked bacon rashers with
    the rinds removed and cut
    into strips
1 medium onion, peeled and
    chopped
1 tbsp chopped fresh lemon
    thyme or basil
1 tbsp chopped fresh parsley
4oz/³⁄₄ cup/100g shredded
    suet
8oz/2 cups/225g fresh
    breadcrumbs
salt and freshly ground black
    pepper
1 egg, beaten*

This recipe was sent to me by Jenny Marsland of Sark in the Channel Islands.

METHOD

Melt the butter in a frying pan (skillet) and fry the bacon until golden brown. Add the onion and fry until soft.

Mix the onions and bacon with the herbs, suet, breadcrumbs, salt and pepper and bind together with the beaten egg.

Bread Sauce

*1oz/2 tbsp/25g butter
2 medium onions, peeled and
    finely chopped*

Bread sauce is the traditional accompaniment to turkey or roast chicken. This eighteenth-century recipe uses a chopped onion and thin cream to make a more flavourful, less stodgy sauce than most modern recipes.

*4oz/1 cup/100g fresh
  breadcrumbs
1/2 pint/1 1/4 cups/300ml
  single (light) cream
salt and freshly ground black
  pepper
pinch of ground cloves*

METHOD

Melt the butter in a pan and gently fry the onions until soft and transparent but not brown. Add the breadcrumbs, cream, salt, pepper and cloves and bring gently to the boil.

Simmer for a few minutes, then remove from the heat and allow to stand for at least 1 hour so that all the flavours blend together.

To serve, bring almost to the boil and pour into a sauceboat.

Celery Sauce

*4 sticks of celery, washed and
  cut into small pieces
3/4 pint/1 3/4 cups/450ml
  turkey or chicken stock
  (bouillon)
1 blade of mace or 1/2 tsp
  ground mace
1 1/2oz/3 tbsp/40g butter
1 1/2oz/6 tbsp/40g plain
  (cake) flour
1/2 pint/1 1/4 cups/300ml milk
salt and freshly ground black
  pepper
2 tbsp double (whipping)
  cream*

This is a nineteenth-century recipe for a sauce that is ideal with roast turkey or chicken.

METHOD

Put the celery, stock (bouillon) and mace into a saucepan. Bring to the boil and simmer for 30 minutes. Put through a liquidizer or food processor or rub through a wire sieve.

Melt the butter in a pan and add the flour. Stir and cook over a moderate heat for 2 minutes. Remove from the heat and gradually add the milk and celery purée. Return to the heat and cook, stirring all the time until the sauce thickens.

Season to taste, stir in the cream and serve immediately.

Cranberry Sauce

*1 pint/2 1/2 cups/600ml fresh
  cranberries
1/4 pint/1/2 cup/150ml water
2oz/just over 1/4 cup/50g
  caster sugar
1/2 wineglass port
1 tbsp redcurrant jelly*

Although cranberries have never been widely grown in Britain, except where they occur naturally in Cumbria, they have been used as an accompaniment to turkey since before the Pilgrim Fathers sailed to America in 1620. The Pilgrim Fathers, however, took the plant with them and grew it in New England, from where it was later exported back to England as an American speciality.

METHOD

Wash the berries in cold water then put into a saucepan with the water. Simmer gently for 30 minutes.

Add the sugar, port and redcurrant jelly and boil again for 2 minutes. The sauce may be eaten as it is, with all the fruit in it, or it can be strained, or puréed in a liquidizer or food processor.

Spiced beef

SERVES 6–8

FOR THE MARINADE

2 cups cider

1 bay leaf

1 tsp cinnamon

1 tsp ground allspice

1 tsp ground cloves

*1 tsp freshly ground black
 pepper*

1½ tsp salt

1 tbsp black treacle (molasses)

½ tbsp brown sugar

*3lb/1.5 kg piece of beef
 topside or silverside*

2 medium onions

2 carrots

1 small turnip

2 stalks of celery

*½ tbsp butter or fat
 (shortening)*

In most parts of Ireland beef, roast, boiled or spiced, has always been the favourite dish for Christmas. Salt beef was eaten almost continuously through the winter, and at Christmas it was spiced as a special treat and took the place of honour on the Christmas table.

METHOD

Mix together all the ingredients for the marinade. Place the meat in a dish and pour the marinade over. Leave for 12 hours, turning the meat twice so that all the meat is coated in marinade.

Place the meat in a heavy saucepan. Combine the marinade with enough water to just cover the meat. Bring to the boil and simmer for 3 hours. Leave to cool.

Meanwhile make the sauce. Peel and chop all the vegetables. Melt the butter or fat (shortening) in a frying pan (skillet) and sauté the vegetables over a moderate heat for 5–10 minutes. Add ¾ pint/ 1¾ cups/400ml of the beef stock (bouillon) and simmer until the vegetables are tender (about 10–15 minutes).

Serve the meat cold and thinly sliced, handing the sauce separately in a sauceboat or jug.

Brawn

SERVES 4–6

1 pig's head

3–4 tbsp salt

4 carrots

2 small turnips

1 medium onion

freshly ground black pepper

a bunch of fresh sweet herbs –
basil, thyme, parsley, a bay
leaf, marjoram

2 blades of mace or 1 tsp
ground mace

4 cloves

12 whole allspice

In the past this was a Staffordshire speciality for Christmas Day. In middle English 'brawn' simply meant meat, particularly boar. 'Brawne with mustard' was mentioned in the menu for a feast served to Richard II at the Bishop of Durham's palace in 1387.

In medieval England the centrepiece of the Christmas table was a boar's head, a relic of the days when it was a sacred dish in many parts of northern Europe. When the boar was slaughtered – usually at the start of winter – the head was salted down and kept for Christmas. It was then boiled gently with vegetables, sage, marjoram and bay leaves, before being glazed and served with mustard.

To make brawn in the past a pig's head was simmered in a large iron pot with the trotters, ears, tail, tongue, bones and gristle, seasoned with herbs and onion skins. When the meat could easily be removed from all the skin and bones, it was arranged neatly in a tin or special mould, and the stock (bouillon) was reduced to almost nothing and poured over it. It was then left to set for 24 hours.

METHOD

Wash the pig's head, sprinkle with salt and leave overnight.

The following day rinse well, place in a large pan with all the other ingredients and cover with cold water. Boil for 2–2½ hours until the meat falls away from the bones. Drain and reserve the liquor.

Cut the meat into small pieces and arrange in a mould. Add a small pinch of cayenne pepper to a little of the liquor and pour over the meat to fill the mould. Leave in the refrigerator to set.

To turn out, dip the outside of the mould into boiling water for 1–2 seconds, then invert on to a serving dish. Garnish with parsley or slices of tomato and cucumber.

Christmas Pudding

MAKES 2 LARGE AND 2 SMALL PUDDINGS

1lb/3 cups/450g raisins

1lb/3 cups/450g sultanas

1lb/3 cups/450g currants

12oz/2 cups/350g mixed
   candied peel

1lb 4oz/3⅜ cups/550g
   shredded suet

6 eggs

1lb/3 cups/450g self-raising
   (all-purpose) flour

1lb/4 cups/450g fresh
   breadcrumbs (white or
   brown or mixed)

1lb/just over 2¼ cups/450g
   demerara sugar

1 tsp grated nutmeg

2 tsp mixed spice

4oz/1¼ cups/100g ground
   almonds

1 pint/2½ cups/600ml barley
   wine or strong ale

½ wineglass of brandy

The solid and very rich Christmas pudding that we eat today is a descendant of a kind of runny porridge that was served at the pagan yuletide festival. The Celtic god of plenty, Dagda (or Dagoderos), was lord of a large cornucopia-like cauldron in which he cooked his porridge of cornmeal, fruit and meat. Dagda's pot was symbolic of the abundance and plenty that would return with the spring, and the gruel was cooked at the winter solstice on 21 December.

The porridge was very similar to frumenty (see page 128) and other gruels that were commonly cooked in medieval days, except that it was made with meat broth. As time went by spices, dried fruits, prunes instead of plums, fruit juices, breadcrumbs and sugar were added to the runny gruel, which was served as part of the main course and eaten with a spoon. Samuel Pepys referred in his diary of 1662 to a 'mess of brave plum porridge'. It was not until the late seventeenth or early eighteenth century that the porridge or pottage became a more solid pudding that was made in the shape of a large football, tied in a floured bag and boiled in a pot over an open fire. By Dickens' day it had become a 'speckled cannonball, so hard and firm, blazing in half of half-a-quartern of ignited brandy . . . ' (from *A Christmas Carol*).

As there are so many different recipes for Christmas pudding I am including here my own family's favourite, which we have been making since the 1920s and possibly longer.

METHOD

Grease 2 large and 2 small pudding bowls.

Mix all the ingredients together until they are evenly distributed and well blended. Turn into the prepared bowls and cover with greaseproof paper. Cover with linen cloths and tie securely with string.

Boil or steam for 8 hours. Store in a cool, dry place. To serve, boil or steam again for 4 hours, then turn out on to a serving dish, decorate with a sprig of holly and pour a ladleful of flaming brandy or rum all over.

Serve with plenty of rum or brandy butter or sauce, and cream.

Brandy Sauce

2 eggs
2oz/just over ¼ cup/50g
    caster sugar
4 tbsp water
1 wineglass of brandy

Some people like a white sauce flavoured with rum or brandy to serve with the Christmas pudding and mince pies, but this is much lighter and creamier, and is perhaps better on the very rich, heavy pudding – especially after a huge plateful of turkey.

METHOD

Beat the eggs, sugar and water in a bowl over a saucepan of boiling water. Add the brandy and continue beating until thick and frothy.

Cumberland Butter

1lb/2 cups/450g unsalted
    butter
8oz/1⅓ cups/225g soft
    brown sugar
a good pinch of grated nutmeg
2 tbsp rum

This is a favourite at Christmas, served with Christmas pudding and mince pies. It also used to play a significant role at births and christenings, for it was eaten by the expectant mother prior to the birth and by any visitors who called to see the new baby, and was also served at the christening feast, spread on biscuits or bread. In Cumberland farmhouses it was known as brown jam or sweet butter. It is essential to use soft brown sugar.

This recipe was sent to me by Pat Hudson of Underbarrow in Cumbria.

METHOD

Soften the butter and beat with the sugar and spice. Gradually add the rum and beat thoroughly. Store in covered jars in a cool place for up to 2 months.

Mince Pies

Mince pies were eaten in Britain long before they became associated with Christmas. The crusading knights brought spices back from the Holy Land, which were used generously in cooking not only to mask the flavour of tainted meats, but also for the pleasure of eating highly seasoned food.

Gradually mince pies became a Christmas delicacy, and before the Reformation they were usually oblong-shaped like a manger and contained a tiny figure of Jesus. When the Puritans forbade all

Christmas activities mince pies had to be eaten in secret. Up to the end of the seventeenth century they were filled with spiced beef, but gradually recipes came to include eggs, raisins, orange or lemon peel, sugar and large quantities of spices, as well as chopped chicken and beef tongue. By the beginning of the nineteenth century the meat content was beginning to disappear, until all that now remains of the original beef ingredient is suet. Cumberland sweet pie (see page 119) is the only Christmas pie that still mixes meat, dried fruits, sugar and spices.

According to old superstition that I found among a hand-written collection of sayings in Cambridge, it is unlucky to be offered a mince pie (you should always ask for one), and every mince pie eaten in a different house between Christmas and New Year indicates a happy and prosperous month in the coming year. It is also unlucky to cut a mince pie with a knife – it should always be broken – and they should only be eaten between Christmas Day and Twelfth Night.

Mince pies are eaten throughout Britain, and each family has its own favourite recipe. Here are two recipes; the second, from Lincolnshire, includes no suet and is therefore suitable for vegetarians. Use the mincemeats to fill little pastry cases made with rich shortcrust pastry (page 132) or rough puff (page 133). Cut circles of pastry 3 inches/8 cm in diameter and use to line little patty tins, fill with mincemeat and cover with lids of pastry cut with a 2 inch 5 cm cutter. Brush the tops with milk or water and sprinkle with caster sugar, then bake for 25–30 minutes at gas 7/220°C/425°F until golden. Serve hot, warm or cold, dredged with more sugar.

1lb/2¾ cups/450g shredded suet

6oz/just over 1 cup/175g raisins

6oz/just over 1 cup/175g sultanas

6oz/just over 1 cup/175g currants

10oz/2–3/275g eating apples, weighed after peeling and coring

10oz/2–3/275g sweet pears, weighed after peeling and coring

10oz/1½ cups/275g demerara sugar

10oz/1⅔ cups/275g mixed candied peel

4oz/1 cup/100g blanched, chopped almonds

½ tsp grated nutmeg

2 tsp mixed spice

finely grated peel and juice of 1 lemon and 1 orange

8 fl oz/1 cup/225ml brandy

4 fl oz/½ cup/100ml sweet sherry

¾ glass maraschino

Hertfordshire Mincemeat

Make this at least a month before Christmas and store in airtight jars. This gives the flavours a chance to blend together and mature.

METHOD
Mix all the ingredients together and store in jars until required.

Vegetarian Mincemeat

*3lb/1.5kg apples, peeled and
  cored*
*2lb/5½ cups/900g demerara
  or soft brown sugar*
4oz/½ cup/100g butter
*1½lb/4½ cups/700g
  currants*
1½lb/4½ cups/700g raisins
*4oz/⅔ cup/100g candied
  mixed peel*
2 tsp grated nutmeg
*finely grated rind and juice of
  1 lemon or orange*

This recipe is from *Recipes from Wrawby*, published by the Lindsey (Lincolnshire) Federation of Women's Institutes.

METHOD

Chop the apples and cook gently until tender. While still hot add the sugar and butter. Mix well then leave to cool.

When cold, add the remaining ingredients and mix thoroughly. Turn into airtight jars, seal and store until required.

Cumberland Sweet Pie

SERVES 8

*rough puff pastry made with
  8oz/2 cups/225g plain
  (cake) flour (see page 133)*
*8oz/225g mutton chops,
  weighed after boning*
8oz/1½ cups/225g currants
8oz/1½ cups/225g sultanas
8oz/1½ cups/225g raisins
6oz/1 cup/175g brown sugar
2oz/⅓ cup/50g candied peel
*juice of 1 large or 2 small
  lemons*
*a pinch each of mace, nutmeg,
  pepper and cinnamon*
½ tsp salt
4 tbsp dark rum
a little stock (bouillon)

This is a popular modern version of the old-fashioned savoury Christmas pie filled with a mixture of meat, dried fruit, spices and sugar. It is traditionally made in Cumbria for the Sunday between Christmas and New Year. Most recipes cook the filling first and then either cover it with a pastry lid or use it to fill a pastry case. As with mincemeat, a little apple is sometimes added for extra moisture.

Seventeenth-century Christmas pies from this part of England sometimes also contained oysters, potatoes, sparrow, dates and chestnuts as well as mutton and all the sweet ingredients.

METHOD

First make the pastry as on page 133 and chill for at least 15 minutes.

Preheat the oven to gas 6/200°C/400°F.

Fill a pie dish with layers of the ingredients, starting with the mutton.

Add the rum and enough stock (bouillon) barely to cover. Cover the dish and bake for 1 hour until the meat is tender.

On a floured board, roll out the pastry and use to cover the pie filling. Bake for 15 minutes then reduce the oven temperature to gas 4/180°C/350°F and bake for a further 20–30 minutes until the pastry is golden and well risen.

Bedfordshire Apple Florentine

SERVES 6

shortcrust pastry made with
    8oz/2 cups/225g plain
    (cake) flour (see page 132)
4 large cooking apples, cored
    and washed
2 tbsp sugar or golden syrup
finely grated rind of 1 lemon
1 pint/2½ cups/600ml ale
a pinch of grated nutmeg
a pinch of ground cinnamon
1 clove
1 tbsp sugar

Apple pies have been a standard Christmas pudding in many places for centuries. This Bedfordshire speciality dates from the eighteenth century and used to be served in a huge pewter dish.

METHOD

First make the pastry as on page 132 and chill for at least 15 minutes.

Preheat the oven to gas 4/180°C/350°F.

Place the whole cored apples in a deep pie dish. Sprinkle with the sugar or syrup and lemon rind.

On a floured board, roll out the pastry and use to cover the apples. Bake for 30 minutes.

Meanwhile heat together, but do not boil, the ale, nutmeg, cinnamon, clove and sugar. When the pie is ready, remove from the oven and carefully lift off the pastry.

Pour the ale mixture over the apples. Cut the pastry into the required number of portions and lay back on top of the apples. Serve immediately.

Christmas Cake

**MAKES AN 8 INCH/20 CM
ROUND CAKE**

1lb/3 cups/450g raisins
1lb/3 cups/450g sultanas
6oz/¾ cup/175g glacé
    cherries
6oz/1 cup/175g mixed
    candied peel
4oz/¾ cup/100g chopped
    dates
4oz/1 cup/100g chopped
    blanched almonds
1 wineglass of whisky or
    brandy
1 tsp grated nutmeg ·
1 tsp mixed spice
1 tsp ground cinnamon

The rich iced fruit cake that every family today either makes or buys for Christmas is a relatively modern development of the yeasted fruit breads that were common throughout Britain until the nineteenth century. Recipes for unyeasted, richer fruit mixtures, using more fruit, spice, eggs and alcohol, started to appear in the middle of the last century.

The marzipan which we use to decorate our cakes underneath the icing was a well-known and widely eaten part of Elizabethan feasts, throughout the year as well as at Christmas (see page 121). The 'marchpane' of those days was used to make iced or gilded fancies, sometimes in elaborate shapes. For the Christmas table in the richest households a single cake or flat tart of marchpane, weighing three or four pounds, was baked and set in the place of honour. It was usually decorated with white icing made from sugar and rosewater, or gilded with gold leaf.

This recipe gives a rich, moist cake that is ideal for weddings, christenings and birthdays as well as Christmas.

*8oz/1 cup/225g butter,
  softened*
*8oz/1¼ cups/225g caster
  sugar*
6 eggs
*12oz/3 cups/350g plain
  (cake) flour*
pinch of salt

METHOD

Preheat the oven to gas 2/150°C/300°F. Line and grease an 8 inch/ 20cm round cake tin.

Mix together the dried fruits and almonds and soak in the whisky or brandy for several hours or overnight.

Add the spices to the fruit. Beat together the butter and sugar until very light and fluffy. Add the eggs, one at a time with a little flour, and beat really hard after each one.

Fold in the remaining flour and salt and mix thoroughly. Add the fruit mixture and blend well together. Turn into the prepared tin and cover with a double layer of greaseproof paper.

Bake for 5–5½ hours. Remove from the oven and leave to cool in the tin overnight. Decorate with marzipan and royal icing.

Marzipan

MAKES ENOUGH FOR 1 × 8 INCH/20 CM ROUND CAKE

*1lb/2 cups/450g granulated
  sugar*
*2.5 fl oz/4½ tbsp/65ml
  water*
*12oz/3¾ cups/350g ground
  almonds*
2 egg whites
*3oz/just under ½ cup/75g
  caster sugar*

Dissolve the sugar in the water and boil to 110°C/240°F or until it forms a soft ball when dropped into cold water. Take the pan off the heat and cool slightly.

Add the almonds and egg whites. Return to a low heat and stir for a few minutes, then turn on to a sugared surface and work in the icing sugar with a palette knife or spatula until the mixture is cool enough to handle. Knead well until smooth.

Wrap and store in an airtight container until required.

Royal Icing

MAKES ENOUGH FOR 1 × 8 INCH 20 CM ROUND CAKE

*1lb/3¾ cups/450g icing
  sugar, sifted*
2 egg whites
1 tsp lemon juice
1 tsp glycerine

Beat the egg whites lightly with a wooden spoon. Add 2 tbsp of icing sugar and beat again. Gradually add the rest of the sugar, beating well to a thick, smooth consistency and a good white colour.

Add the lemon juice and glycerine and beat again (the glycerine stops the icing from becoming too brittle). Use immediately or cover with a damp cloth until required.

Pepper Cakes

These are a Christmas favourite in the north of England, and used to be popular throughout the country. An eighteenth-century recipe makes them from white peppercorns, sherry and icing sugar, and this mixture gave a sort of fondant-like sweetmeat. More recent recipes sometimes use pepper, but generally they are flavoured with ginger and cloves. In the north, the cakes are often given to carol singers with a glass of some warming beverage.

Some recipes include currants and raisins but they are more commonly crisp, plain biscuits (cookies) cut with pastry cutters, or squares cut, as with this recipe, from a cake baked in a square tin.

MAKES 16 SQUARES

12oz/3 cups/350g plain (cake) flour

2oz/¹⁄₃ cup/50g soft brown sugar

¹⁄₂ tsp ground cloves

¹⁄₂ tsp ground ginger

4oz/¹⁄₂ cup/100g butter, softened

¹⁄₂ tsp bicarbonate of soda dissolved in a little milk

2 eggs, beaten

12oz/8 tbsp/350g dark treacle (molasses)

METHOD

Preheat the oven to gas 3/170°C/325°F. Grease and line an 8 inch/20 cm square tin.

Mix together the flour, sugar and spices. Rub or cut in the butter. Add the dissolved bicarbonate of soda, the eggs and treacle (molasses) and mix thoroughly together.

Turn into the prepared tin and bake for 1½–2 hours until a warm skewer comes out clean. Remove from the oven and leave to cool in the tin. When cold, turn out, wrap and store for at least 1 week before cutting into 16 squares.

Clapshot

SERVES 6–8

1lb/450g potatoes

1lb/450g turnips

This is a very well-known Orkney dish, served with haggis at Hogmanay and on Burns Night. It is very similar to all the potato dishes cooked in Ireland and Scotland at Hallowe'en, and is

*salt and freshly ground black
    pepper*
2 tbsp fresh chopped chives
1oz/2 tbsp/25g butter

absolutely delicious with any meat. Haggis originates from Greece. The Greeks apparently passed the recipe to the Romans and from Rome it travelled to France. The French named it 'Hacher', from which the Scottish name is supposed to derive. It arrived in Scotland in about 1600. I have not included a recipe for haggis, as it is much easier and pleasanter to buy a ready-made haggis from a butcher's shop or specialist food store.

METHOD

Peel the potatoes and turnips and cut into small pieces. Boil in salted water for 15–20 minutes until soft. Drain and mash together then beat with the pepper, chives and butter until fluffy.

Although they are not traditional ingredients I also add about 1oz/2 tbsp/25g cream cheese or 1 tbsp double (whipping) cream to make a very creamy mixture. Serve very hot.

Roast Venison

SERVES 4

*salt and freshly ground black
    pepper*
½ tsp ground mace
½ tsp ground cinnamon
½ tsp grated nutmeg
2lb/900g piece of venison
¼ pint/½ cup/150ml claret
*¼ pint/½ cup/150ml good
    wine vinegar*
2oz/4 tbsp/50g butter, melted
*2–3 tbsp plain (cake) flour
    for dredging*
*½ pint/1¼ cups/300ml meat
    stock (bouillon)*
*2 tbsp walnut ketchup
    (catsup)*

Venison was a favourite meat in Scotland for St Andrew's Day, Burns Night, Hogmanay and other Scottish national dinners. It was often roasted and served with wine sauce and currant jelly, and sometimes with barley and oat pudding. At Hogmanay the meat was usually served cold in slices with oatcakes and butter.

METHOD

Mix together the salt, pepper, mace, cinnamon and nutmeg and rub into the venison. Cover with the claret and vinegar and leave to marinate for at least 6 hours or overnight.

Heat the oven to gas 5/190°C/375°F. Strain the liquor from the meat and add to it the melted butter. Use this mixture to baste the meat while it is roasting.

Place the venison in a roasting dish and cook for 45 minutes. Remove from the oven, baste with the butter mixture and dredge with plain (cake) flour. Return to the oven and cook for a further 15 minutes. Remove from the oven and lift the meat on to a serving dish. Keep hot.

For the gravy, boil together the meat stock (bouillon), the contents of the roasting dish and the walnut ketchup (catsup). Pour over the meat or serve separately in a sauceboat or jug.

Black Bun

MAKES 1 × 7 INCH/
17.5 CM CAKE

FOR THE PASTRY

12oz/3 cups/350g plain
   (cake) flour
pinch of salt
3oz/6 tbsp/75g butter,
   softened
2 tbsp sugar
2 eggs, lightly beaten
4–6 tbsp iced water

FOR THE FILLING

8oz/2 cups/225g plain (cake)
   flour
1 tsp bicarbonate of soda
1½ tsp baking powder
4oz/²/3 cup/100g soft brown
   sugar
2 tsp mixed spice
½ tsp ground cinnamon
½ tsp ground ginger
½ tsp ground mace
12oz/just over 2 cups/350g
   sultanas or raisins
12oz/just over 2 cups/350g
   currants
4oz/1 cup/100g blanched
   chopped almonds
4oz/1 cup/100g chopped
   walnuts
4oz/²/3 cup/100g mixed
   candied peel
grated rind and juice of 1
   lemon
6 fl oz/3/4 cup/175 ml milk
1 tbsp brandy
1 egg, beaten

This is a very rich fruit cake baked in a pastry crust for Hogmanay. Like Cumberland sweet pie and mince pies, it is a descendant of the dough-crusted raised pies that were once traditional Christmas fare. It is much darker and richer than an English Christmas cake. During Hogmanay first-footers were given the first slice of black bun with a glass of whisky or Athole brose.

The cake is usually made at least two weeks before New Year to give the mixture a chance to mature.

METHOD

First make the pastry. Sift together the flour and salt. Add the butter and rub or cut in until the mixture resembles fine breadcrumbs. Stir in the sugar.

Add the eggs with 4 tbsp iced water and mix into the flour using a round-bladed knife. Use a little more water if necessary. Knead the dough gently then wrap in foil or cling film and chill for at least 30 minutes.

Grease a 7 inch/17.5 cm round tin. Divide the dough into 2 pieces, one slightly smaller than the other (for the pastry lid). On a lightly floured board roll out the larger piece of dough to a circle approximately ½ inch/1 cm thick.

Ease the circle of pastry gently into the prepared tin and press down to line the bottom and sides. Trim off any excess dough and put into the refrigerator to chill.

Meanwhile, preheat the oven to gas 6/200°C/400°F and make the filling. Sift together the flour, bicarbonate of soda and baking powder. Add the sugar, spice, dried fruit, nuts, lemon juice and rind. Mix well.

Add the milk and brandy and mix thoroughly until all the ingredients are evenly distributed. Spoon the filling into the pastry case and press flat.

On a lightly floured board roll out the smaller piece of dough to a circle to fit the top of the cake. Dampen the edges of the dough with a little milk or water and lay over the filling. Press the edges well together. Trim off any excess dough and brush the top with beaten egg.

Bake for 15 minutes then remove the tin from the oven and cover with tinfoil. Return to the oven, reduce the temperature to gas 3/170°C/325°F and continue baking for a further 3½ hours until a warm skewer comes out clean.

Remove from the oven and turn out carefully on to a wire rack to cool. When cold, wrap well in tinfoil or cling film and store in an airtight tin for at least 1 week.

Shortbread

Shortbread has its origins in Roman marriage rites, when it was the custom to break a wheaten cake over the head of the bride. The cake therefore had to be of a light, crumbly texture so that it broke easily. 'Short' implies that the mixture contains fat (shortening), and the more fat there is the shorter and more crumbly the cake.

Today it is very much a Scottish speciality. Every household in Scotland bakes shortbread for Hogmanay using only the very best ingredients. Petticoat tails, the best-known form, date from the twelfth century, when they were known as 'petty cotes tallis', meaning little cases or containers (cotes as in dove-cotes) made of pastry, cut into triangular pieces and filled. Tallis (or tallys) were cuts made in a stick to keep a record or measure, and came to mean any cut-out pattern. The traditional shortbread always had a small circle cut separately in the centre so that the points of the individual pieces would not crumble off and be wasted when the segments were divided.

Petticoat Tails

MAKES 8 OR 12 PIECES

7oz/1¾ cups/200g plain (cake) flour
2oz/just under ½ cup/50g icing sugar
3oz/6 tbsp/75g butter, softened
1oz/2 tbsp/25g lard, softened
2–3 tsp caraway seeds (optional)
caster sugar for dredging

Preheat the oven to gas 4/180°C/350°F. Grease a baking tray.

Sift together the flour and icing sugar. Rub or cut in the butter and lard until the mixture resembles fine breadcrumbs. Mix in the caraway seeds, if using.

Turn the dough out on to a lightly floured board and knead until firm but pliable. On the prepared baking tray, roll the dough out to a round approximately ¼ inch/0.5 cm thick.

Crimp the edges neatly with finger and thumb and prick all over with the prongs of a fork or a skewer. Mark a circle in the middle and mark the rest into 8 or 12 pieces.

Bake for 20–30 minutes until pale golden. Remove from the oven and dredge with caster sugar while still hot.

Scottish Shortbread

MAKES 8 OR 12 PIECES

8oz/1 cup/225g butter,
*   softened*
4oz/⁵⁄₈ cup/100g caster sugar
8oz/2 cups/225g plain (cake)
*   flour*
4oz/³⁄₄ cup/100g rice flour
blanched almonds or strips of
*   lemon or orange peel to*
*   decorate*

This mixture gives a softer, crumblier shortbread than petticoat tails, which should be crisp.

METHOD

Preheat the oven to gas 5/190°C/375°F. Grease 2 × 7 inch/17.5 cm round sandwich tins.

Beat together the butter and sugar until light and creamy. Mix together the flour and rice flour and gradually work into the butter and sugar mixture. Work together very lightly with the finger tips. (The less handling the better to prevent the dough from becoming too oily.)

Press the mixture into the prepared tins and smooth the top. Prick all over with the prongs of a fork or a skewer. Mark into 8 or 12 pieces and decorate the top with almonds or thin strips of lemon or orange peel.

Bake for 5-10 minutes then reduce the heat to gas 3/170°C/325°F and bake for a further 8–10 minutes until a pale golden colour. Remove from the oven and leave to cool in the tin. When cold, turn out and cut along the marked lines.

Twelfth Cake

MAKES 1 × 10 INCH/25 CM ROUND CAKE

8oz/1 cup/225g butter, softened

8oz/1 cup/225g sugar

4 eggs

8oz/2 cups/225g plain (cake) flour

2 tsp mixed spice

6oz/just over 1 cup/175g currants

8oz/1½ cups/225g sultanas

2oz/⅓ cup/50g mixed candied peel

2oz/¼ cup/50g glacé cherries (halved)

2–3 tbsp brandy or rum

1 dried pea and 1 dried bean

The ceremonies that took place on Twelfth Day were of Roman origin and the focus of the day was a huge feast when the last of the Christmas boar or pig was garnished and served up, or made into an elaborate pie. There was also a large plum cake which contained a hidden bean and a pea. Whoever found these became King or Queen of Misrule and presided over the night's revels. By the late eighteenth century the cake had become a rich fruit cake, elaborately iced and decorated with bright-coloured sugar flowers, gold stars, crowns, angels and figures of the three kings at Bethlehem. In Hampshire Twelfth Night was called 'Feast of the Stars', and the cake was iced with blue for the sky and decorated with silver stars and twelve candles. In London a Twelfth cake is served annually to the company of actors and actresses performing at the Theatre Royal in Drury Lane, London. This is the Baddeley cake, endowed in the will of Robert Baddeley, a pastry cook turned actor, who died in 1794.

METHOD

Preheat the oven to gas 2/150°C/300°F. Grease and line a 10 inch/25 cm round tin.

Beat together the butter and sugar until light and fluffy. Beat in the eggs, one at a time with 1 tbsp of flour with each egg. Beat hard.

Add the rest of the flour, the mixed spice, the dried fruit and the brandy or rum and mix thoroughly so that all the ingredients are evenly distributed.

Turn into the prepared tin and smooth the top, leaving the middle slightly hollowed out. Insert the pea and the bean.

Tie a double layer of brown paper or thick greaseproof paper round the tin and bake for 3–3½ hours until a warm skewer comes out clean. If the top of the cake starts to become too brown cover with brown or greaseproof paper.

Remove from the oven and leave to cool in the tin for 15 minutes. Turn out on to a wire rack to cool completely before decorating.

Frumenty

SERVES 3–4

1 pint/2½ cups/600ml cree'd wheat

1 pint/2½ cups/600ml milk

2 tbsp raisins

a little grated nutmeg or cinnamon

2 or 3 beaten egg yolks mixed with a little cold milk

sugar or honey to taste

a little rum or brandy, or double cream (optional)

Frumenty was commonly eaten for breakfast or perhaps as a pudding in many counties of Britain until the 1930s at Christmas, New Year, for Mothering Sunday and other special occasions through the year. In some places the cree'd or fermented wheat that forms the basis of this dish was sold in the street or ordered by post in special tins. Since the cree'd wheat is made with the whole grain of wheat, with only the outer husk removed, it is an excellent source of vitamins A and B.

TO PREPARE WHEAT FOR FRUMENTY

Wash some new wheat with the outside husk removed thoroughly and put into a pan with three times its own volume of cold water. Set on a very low heat (an Aga is ideal) for 24 hours until it is quite soft. When cold the mixture becomes a jelly with the burst cooked wheat grains in it and this is called cree'd wheat.

TO PREPARE FRUMENTY FOR THE TABLE

In a large pan mix the wheat with the milk and bring to the boil, stirring from time to time. When it begins to thicken add the raisins and spice. Add the egg yolks and cook gently until thick and creamy. Just before serving stir in the sugar or honey, with the rum, brandy or cream, if using, to taste. (If preferred, instead of using egg yolks, the frumenty may be thickened with a little plain (cake) flour mixed with a little milk.)

Athole Brose

6oz/just over 1 cup/175g medium oatmeal

¼ pint/½ cup/150ml water

2 tbsp heather honey

1½ pints/3¾ cups/900ml whisky

This is a very old Scottish drink brewed for Hogmanay celebrations in the Highlands. The oatmeal in the old recipe meant that the drink served a double purpose at Hogmanay, providing not only alcoholic stimulation but also some sustenance through the night of revels and festivities. The drink was sometimes given as a cure for a cold.

The word 'brose' was usually attached to dishes made from oatmeal. The earliest brose is thought to have been a cold drink made from oats or barley meal mixed with water, probably from a mountain stream or spring, and carried in flasks by farmers, shepherds and workmen. The warmth of the body and the movement probably helped to ferment the mixture so that it became a bubbly, sweet, thin, batter-like gruel that was very nourishing and quite intoxicating. Today the word brose means almost any kind of broth.

METHOD

Put the oatmeal into a small bowl and add the water. Mix to a paste and leave for 1 hour, then press through a wire sieve.

Add the honey to the strained liquid and mix thoroughly. Pour into a large bottle and fill with the whisky. Shake well before drinking.

Wassail Bowl (Lamb's Wool)

SERVES 8–10

8 red eating apples

16 cloves

1 gall/20 cups/4.4 litres ale

1 inch/2.5cm stick of cinnamon

6 whole allspice

1 tsp grated nutmeg

½ tsp ginger

2 tbsp sugar

The word 'wassail' derives from the Anglo-Saxon *wes hal*, meaning be in good health, a greeting at festive times and especially at Christmas time, when groups of people would go from house to house singing songs of Christmas cheer and good wishes. This wassailing was often practised during the last days of advent and right through the twelve days of Christmas to Twelfth Night. The wassailers would usually carry with them a large wooden bowl or cup filled with a frothing brew called lamb's wool, which they offered to passers-by or the local residents.

In most regions the wassail bowl usually contains roasted apples that float in the spiced beer, and in Wales it also contains cakes. Cakes and roast apples were set in rows on top of each other with sugar sprinkled between, and then the warm beer and spices were added. As elsewhere, friends sat in a circle and passed the bowl from hand to hand. In some places each person took an apple with a spoon and drank from the bowl. In others the beer was drunk first then the cakes and apples were eaten.

In some places the date for wassailing is 17 January, or Old Twelfth Night. In Hampshire and parts of the west country this was the day for wassailing the apple orchards to ensure a good crop in the coming year. In every orchard the most ancient tree was surrounded and sporting guns were fired up into the branches to frighten away evil spirits. The youngest person then climbed up into the tree and fixed there a piece of cake or bread soaked in cider, and a bucket of cider was poured over the roots of the tree while a prayer was said to the tree spirit. The wassailers then joined hands around the tree and sang a special apple wassail song. There are a few places where the ceremony still takes place today.

The name lamb's wool is thought to derive from 'La Masubal' the name given to a day dedicated to a deity of fruits and seeds, symbols of fruitfulness and health. The drink therefore has strong links with wassailing, and was commonly drunk around Britain on saints' days, harvest, Hallowe'en and other festive occasions.

METHOD

Wash the apples and stick the cloves into the skin. Heat the oven to gas 6/200°C/400°F and roast the apples in a little water for 30 minutes until the flesh is tender but not mushy.

Heat the ale in a large pan with the sugar and spices until almost boiling, but do not allow to boil.

Place the apples into a large punch bowl or tureen and pour the frothing ale over them.

Although not traditional, beaten eggs and thick cream may be added to the mixture just before pouring over the apples.

Wassail Bowl

RECIPE ON PAGE 129

Pastry Recipes

Flaky Pastry

1lb/4 cups/450g plain flour,
  sifted
½ tsp salt
12oz/1½ cups/350g butter or
  half butter and half lard
1 tsp lemon juice
½ pint/1¼ cups/600ml cold
  water

Mix together the flour and salt. Divide the fat into 4 portions. Rub or cut 1 portion into the flour. Mix in the lemon juice and cold water and bind together to a soft dough. Knead lightly on a floured board until really smooth. Roll out the dough to a rectangle 3 times longer than wide. Use the second portion of fat to dot the top two thirds of the dough. Fold up the bottom third and fold down the top third of the dough. Seal the edges with the rolling pin and wrap in a plastic bag and chill for 15 minutes in the refrigerator. Place the dough on a floured board and, with the folded edges to your left and right, roll out into a long strip again. Repeat the dotting with the third portion of fat, folding and chilling again. Repeat the whole process once more with the remaining fat. Wrap again and chill for ¾–1 hour before using.

Shortcrust Pastry

8oz/2 cups/225g plain flour
a pinch of salt
2oz/4 tbsp/50g margarine or
  butter, softened
2oz/4 tbsp/50g lard, softened
2 tbsp cold water

Mix the flour and salt together. Rub or cut in the fat until the mixture resembles fine breadcrumbs. Gradually add enough water to give a stiff but pliable dough. Knead lightly for a few minutes but do not overknead as this can make the pastry tough. Wrap in cling-wrap and chill in the refrigerator for at least 15 minutes.

Rich Shortcrust Pastry

8oz/2 cups/225g plain flour,
  sifted
a good pinch of salt
6oz/¾ cup/175g butter,
  softened
1 medium egg yolk
2 tsp caster sugar
1–2 tbsp cold water

Mix together the flour and salt. Rub or cut in the butter until the mixture resembles fine breadcrumbs. Make a well in the middle and add the egg yolk and sugar. Mix with a round-bladed knife and add enough water to give a soft pliable dough. Knead lightly, wrap in cling-wrap and chill in the refrigerator for at least 15 minutes.

Rough Puff Pastry

8oz/2 cups/225g plain flour
a pinch of salt
6oz/³⁄4 cup/175g butter, or
* half butter and half lard,*
* softened*
¹⁄2 tsp lemon juice
2–3 tbsp cold water

Mix together the flour and salt. Cut the fat into walnut-sized pieces and stir lightly into the flour with a round-bladed knife. Make a well in the middle and mix in the lemon juice and enough water to give an elastic dough. On a floured board, roll out the dough to a long strip, keeping the corners as square as possible, and the sides straight. Fold the bottom third up and the top third down and turn the dough so that the folded edges are on your left and right. Repeat the rolling and folding process three more times, leaving, if possible, 15 minutes between the second and third and between the third and fourth rolling. Wrap in cling-wrap and chill for at least 15 minutes before using.

Hot Water Crust

8oz/2 cups/225g plain flour
1 tsp salt
2¹⁄2oz/5 tbsp/65g lard
4 fl oz/¹⁄2 cup/100ml milk or
* water*

Sift the flour and salt into a warm bowl and make a well in the middle. Keep warm. Gently heat the lard and milk or water together until boiling. Pour into the well in the flour and mix well with a wooden spoon. When cool enough to handle, knead thoroughly with floured hands. Leave covered in a warm place for ¹⁄2 hour. Use immediately. Do not allow the dough to become too warm or it will be too soft and pliable to be workable. It must be able to retain its shape and support its own weight.

TO RAISE A PIE

The pastry must be raised or moulded while warm. Keep back ¹⁄4 for the lid and leave in a bowl in a warm place covered with a cloth. Roll out the remainder to a thickness of about ¹⁄4 inch/.5cm to a round or oval shape. Mould the pastry with the hands to form the base and sides of the pie. When cold and set put in the filling. Roll out the lid, dampen the eges of the case, put on the lid and press the edges firmly together. Pin 3 or 4 thicknesses of greaseproof paper round the outside during baking to hold the shape and prevent burning.

BREARS, Peter, *Traditional Food in Yorkshire*, 1987, John Donaldson.

BRIDGE, Tom, *Lancashire Recipes Old and New*, 1985, Dalesman.

COURTNEY, Margaret, *Cornish Feasts and Folk Lore*, 1890, E. P. Publishers Ltd.

DOUGLAS, Joyce, *Old Derbyshire Recipes and Customs*, 1976, Hendon Publishing Co. Ltd.

ELDER, Eileen, *Lincolnshire Country Food*, 1985, Scunthorpe Borough Museum & Art Gallery.

ELLIS, Audrey, *Traditional British Cooking*, 1979, Hamlyn.

FAIRLIE, Margaret, *Traditional Scottish Cookery*, 1975, Hale.

FITZGIBBON, Theodora, *A Taste of Yorkshire*, 1979, Pan Books
  A Taste of the Lake District, 1980, Ward Lock.
  Traditional Scottish Cookery, 1980, Fontana.
  Traditional West Country Cookery, 1982, Collins & Co. Ltd, Fontana.
  Irish Traditional Food, 1983, Gill and Macmillan.

FREEMAN, Bobby, *Welsh Country Cookery*, 1988, Y Lolfa.

HARTLEY, Dorothy, *Food in England*, 1954, Macdonald & Co – Futura.

HEATON, Nell, *Traditional Recipes of the British Isles*, 1951, Faber & Faber.

IRWIN, Florence, *The Cookin' Woman*, 1986, The Blackstaff Press.

MACFAYDEN, David, and HOLE, Christina, *The Folk Customs of Britain*, 1983, Hutchinson.

McNEILL, Marian, *The Scots Kitchen*, 1929, Blackie.

OWEN, Trefor, *Welsh Folk Customs*, 1974, Gomer Press.

POULSON, Joan, *Old Northern Recipes*, 1975, Hendon Publishing Co. Ltd.
  Old Anglian Recipes, 1976, Hendon Publishing Co. Ltd.
  Old Cotswold Recipes, 1976, Hendon Publishing Co. Ltd.
  Old Thames Valley Recipes, 1977, Hendon Publishing Co. Ltd.
  North Country Traditions, 1977, Hendon Publishing Co. Ltd.
  Lakeland Recipes Old and New, 1978, Countryside Publications.
  Yorkshire Cookery, 1979, Batsford.
  Traditional North Country Recipes, 1985, Cicerone.

SHARKEY, Olive, *Old Days Old Ways*, 1985, O'Brien, Dublin.

SLACK, Margaret, *Yorkshire Fare*, 1979, Dalesman.
  Northumbrian Fare, 1981, Frank Graham.

THOMSON, George, *Traditional Irish Recipes*, 1982, Canongate, Edinburgh.

WHITE, Florence, *Good Things in England*, 1932, Jonathan Cape.

WHITLOCK, Ralph, *A Calendar of Country Customs*, 1978, Batsford.

WOOLLEY, Suzanne, *My Grandmother's Cookery Book*, 1975, Shearwater Press Ltd.

WRIGHT, Mary, *Cornish Treats*, 1986, Alison Hodge.